D. Edmond von Adelung
1925

From

C. M. Wandle

april 16/25

THOMAS STARR KING
Patriot and Preacher

T. S. King

THOMAS STARR KING

PATRIOT AND PREACHER

BY

CHARLES W. WENDTE

Nationality and Humanity are equally sacred.
To forget humanity is to suppress the aim of
our labors; to cancel the nation is to suppress
the instrument by which to achieve the aim.

JOSEPH MAZZINI.

THE BEACON PRESS

BOSTON -:- MASSACHUSETTS

19915

TO
DAVID STARR JORDAN
IN
ADMIRATION AND FRIENDSHIP

TABLE OF CONTENTS

LIST OF ILLUSTRATIONS

FOREWORD

My first acquaintance with Thomas Starr King was when, in the spring of 1861, a youth of seventeen, accompanied by my widowed mother and younger brother, I arrived in San Francisco, by way of the Isthmus of Panama, in search of health and opportunity. Our family physician had warned me to exchange at once the harsh climate of my native city of Boston for the sunshine and out-of-door life of California. I had little or no acquaintance with conditions on the Pacific Coast. My only reliance was on the Providence which had hitherto guided our family destinies, and my earnest purpose and modest capacity for service. Kind friends had provided me with letters of introduction to residents of San Francisco. One of these addressed to the Rev. Thomas Starr King of that city proved to be the golden key which not only opened to me the riches of his opulent and generous nature, but also the door of social, business and religious opportunity.

On landing, our little family found a temporary abiding place. The next step was to present our letters of introduction and seek some bread-winning employment.

I was fortunate enough to secure employment for a few weeks as Secretary of the San Francisco Board of Port Wardens, a position which had become vacant. At the close of this brief term, however, the Democratic incumbents would go out of office, the Union party having triumphed at the recent state election. The incoming governor, Hon. Leland Stanford, would have the appointment of the new board and its secretary. The duties of the latter office proved to be congenial and not exacting. The salary attached to the place would enable me to support my mother and myself and put an end to our domestic anxiety. The desire to retain the position naturally arose. But I had rendered no party service whatever, and hence, according to the political ethics of that day, had no claim on the office. Only one possibility remained. Thomas Starr King, who had come to California the year previous, had already made himself widely influential through his eloquence and patriotism. The recent success of the Union cause at the polls was in no slight degree attributable to him. The incoming governor was his personal friend and parishioner. If now Mr. King were to ask for this small post for me it would surely not be denied him. But could a newcomer like myself, known to him only through a letter of introduction, venture to ask such a favor? The necessities of the situation made me bold. Mr. King had received me kindly and expressed an interest in our family fortunes. He and his wife had called upon us. He had inquired about my studies and aims in life. I felt encouraged, therefore, to appeal to the man whose discourses on Sunday and expressions of personal good-will had given me an exalted idea of his intellectual and moral qualities and his goodness of heart.

Mr. King received me with cordiality, and listened sympathetically to my story and timid suggestion of his possible ability to aid me in this critical juncture of my life. He assured me of his readiness to do all in his power to further my aim, and that he felt particularly drawn to it because he himself when a youth of sixteen had secured a similar office in the Charlestown Navy Yard, which had enabled him to support his mother and sister for some years until he entered his present profession. He felt he had been of some aid to the Union cause in California by his public addresses. Governor Stanford was to be in town the very next day. He would call upon him and ask my appointment. It was very uncertain. The position might already be disposed of. I must indulge in no undue hopes. He would do his best for me. It was arranged that I should call on Mr. King in the evening of the next day and learn the result of his interview with the Governor.

The next day was an anxious one. So much depended on its issue for me and mine. At noon a terrific storm burst over the city. The rain fell in torrents, overflowing the lower streets, while the surging waters of the bay swept over the wharves. Alone in the office, I mechanically put the records in the safe and waited for the fury of the storm to subside

[xiii]

before venturing homeward. I was indescribably
sad. My usual hopefulness had entirely deserted me.
Suddenly I was surprised to hear a sharp rap at the
door. I opened it, and there without, to my amazement, stood Starr King, his cheeks flushed, his luminous eyes filled with joy, and his hand extended as he
cried: "It's all right, my boy! It's all right! I've
seen Governor Stanford. He was very cordial, and
you are to retain your position for the two years of
his administration. I congratulate you. I'm so
glad!" But I, though rejoicing at the happy news,
could see only the rain-drops that dripped from his
long, lank hair and saturated garments: "O, Mr.
King, why did you come so far in such a deluge to
tell me this? Why, I was to call on you this evening
and learn my fate!" "Never mind, my dear fellow.
It's only a little rain—my umbrella was blown to
bits at the corner. I knew you must be very anxious
to learn the result of my interview with the Governor,
so I came right down to tell you. I thought I might
make you happy a few hours earlier."

Such was Starr King! It is no wonder that the
men and women, both East and West, who had the
privilege of his friendship were attached to him with
a devotion which neither death nor the lapse of years
can diminish, and treasure his memory with gratitude,
as an inspiration for their higher faith in goodness
and an incentive to nobler living.

The narration of this incident, which in his early
manhood brought the writer close to the generous

heart of Starr King, will make better understood the
tribute to that eminent man which follows this introduction. The friendly regard thus displayed at the
outset Mr. King continued to show throughout the
remainder of his brief life on earth, with an ever-
increasing veneration on the part of the younger man
for the brilliant gifts, the public services and personal
character of his pastor and friend. Just before Mr.
King's lamented death, as I afterwards learned, he
had interceded with the new governor-elect, that I
might retain my position, a request which was
granted. The whole tenor of my life was changed
and determined by my acquaintance with Starr King.
I eagerly availed myself of my opportunities to hear
him preach and lecture, listening with delight to his
great orations in behalf of the Union and the Constitution in that critical hour of American, and especially of Californian history. I sought his society
and counsel. His death was the first great sorrow
of my life, and the impression produced upon me by
his character and career so profound, that not long
after I decided to give up all thoughts of a business
future and devote myself to the vocation of a Liberal
Christian minister. Returning to the East I gradu-
ated from the Harvard Divinity School in 1869 with
the fixed purpose of returning to California to labor
for the ideal causes which Starr King had represented
in his life and ministry. But it was not until nearly
twenty years later that I was enabled to carry out
these plans. Returning to the Pacific States for

[xv]

twelve years of ministerial and public service, I sought everywhere and always to magnify the personality and career of Starr King as the type of religion and citizenship demanded by the young civilization of the Coast.

It was a privilege to renew acquaintance with the surviving family and friends of Mr. King, and especially to take an active part in the popular movement to honor his memory which led to the erection, in 1892, of a noble statue and monument to this Christian patriot of California in the great public park of San Francisco which overlooks the Golden Gate, and at whose unveiling I uttered the dedicatory prayer.

One other service I fain would have rendered the memory of my friend, the preparation of an adequate biography of him, for which I had begun to collect materials.

His surviving family were divided in opinion as to the advisability of a more extended life of Mr. King than the admirable but all too brief memoir by Edwin P. Whipple which had been prefixed, at their instance, to the published collection of Mr. King's orations and discourses.

In the meantime the interest in Mr. King's career and public services has not diminished but increased. Constant references are made to his personal gifts and qualities, and his religious and patriotic activities during the great Civil War as one of the moral founders of the new Commonwealth of California. Various addresses and monographs have appeared on the

FOREWORD

subject. In my own case a lecture on this congenial theme has been delivered all over the Eastern and Western States of the Union. The interest it has called forth, especially in these recent years of world war for freedom, righteousness and democracy, has encouraged the writer to amplify and put into permanent form this personal tribute to the hero of his younger days. The narrative is enriched by the inclusion of as yet unpublished letters of Mr. King to his friends: also by extracts from Mr. King's journal of his voyage, via the Isthmus of Panama, in 1860, to San Francisco, and his letters to the *Boston Evening Transcript* on California scenery and life, as well as by illustrative citations from his writings.

The author ventures to hope that these features may contribute to a fuller knowledge and better appreciation of this champion of Nationality as the appointed way to World-Brotherhood, and of Patriotism as an exalted virtue of individual character and civil society, and so help to inspire a future generation, as it has aided in redeeming a past one.

Acknowledgments are due to many friends who have aided his undertaking, especially to Miss Florence Cushman, a niece, and the Misses Wiggin, of Newton, relatives of Starr King.

CHARLES W. WENDTE.

PART I
THOMAS STARR KING

THOMAS STARR KING

CHAPTER I

ANTECEDENTS AND EDUCATION

THOMAS STARR KING, patriot and preacher of Civil War fame, lying on his death-bed in San Francisco in the fortieth year of his age, said sadly, as he thought of his friends on the other side of the continent: "To-day is the fourth of March. Sad news will go over the wires to-day." A few moments later, after a touching farewell to his family and friends about his bedside, with avowals of trust in the Eternal and full assurance of immortal life, this champion of country and humanity passed calmly away, leaving not only his friends, but the state, the nation, in sorrow at the loss of one of the most eloquent advocates of the national idea and the virtues of patriotism in American history.

There is no danger that those among the living who were permitted to know Mr. King personally and were eye-witnesses of his public career will ever forget that gifted and radiant being. They treasure the memory of his unspotted life, his ardent love of country, and his eloquent appeals for the preserva-

[3]

tion of the Union and the emancipation of the slave. They do not cease to mourn the early death which came to him because of his utter devotion to the undivided nation and the public honor and welfare.

But a new generation has come into being since those crucial days of the republic, to whom the name of Starr King is only a tradition vaguely associated with eloquent utterances and patriotic service rendered the State of California during the Civil War of 1860–65. To inform these more fully concerning this leader of the national sentiment, and thus help preserve his influence in our American democracy, is the purpose of this tribute to Starr King by one who was his contemporary in California, who knew him personally, and was an admiring witness of his public activities. For, as Starr King himself told us in an early lecture on George Washington, if we cannot have *sight* of great men it is well that we should learn what we can of their character and career, and take their example to heart as an incentive to equal devotion.

Certainly no public man associated with the early history of California better deserves this recognition. More than any other citizen Starr King assured the loyalty and preserved the internal peace of California in the critical hour of her history, and was the eloquent voice of her patriotism, the eulogist of her magnificent scenery, the quickener of her intellectual life, the prophet of her coming greatness, and the type of her broad, humanitarian religion.

[4]

ANTECEDENTS AND EDUCATION

Starr King had already a national reputation when he came to California in the spring of 1860 as minister-elect of the Unitarian Society in San Francisco. Looking back on his personal history it is interesting to note that his immediate ancestry on the maternal side was German, his maternal grandfather, Thomas Starr, having emigrated from the Rhine lands to the United States, with his wife and son Thomas, in the latter part of the eighteenth century. This son Thomas became a business man in New York City and married Mary Lavinus of French descent. Their second daughter, Susan Starr, married Rev. Thomas Farrington King, of English antecedents, whose eldest child was Thomas Starr King, born in New York City on December 17th, 1824. Thus three nations contributed to his endowment.

The father was a man of high character, good abilities as a preacher and fine social qualities. From him "Starr" inherited his sunny disposition, keen sense of humor and companionable nature. His intellectual gifts seem to have descended to him chiefly through his mother, a woman of character and intelligence, who early noted and sedulously fostered the studious bent of her talented son. His father, settled at first in Hudson, N. Y., accepted an invitation to become pastor of a Universalist Society in Portsmouth, N. H., and in this picturesque old seaport Starr passed six years of his boyhood. He was sent to a private school where, besides the usual

[5]

branches of study, he acquired a good knowledge, for his age, of Latin and French. In 1835 the family removed to Charlestown, Mass., whither Rev. Mr. King had been called as pastor of a large Universalist church, and here Starr spent his youth and early manhood. He was educated in the excellent public schools of Charlestown, whose residents in that day were chiefly of American stock, and whose proximity to Boston and Cambridge imparted an unusual degree of culture to its society, while the traditions clustering about Bunker Hill and the early struggle for national independence made it one of the shrines and nurseries of American patriotism. There being no high school in the town, an arrangement was made by which pupils could be fitted for college under the excellent tuition of the principal of the grammar school, Mr. Joshua Bates. Starr's manifest ability, graceful and impressive declamation and talented compositions attracted the attention of his teachers and indicated his future distinction. He seemed mature beyond his years, while his sincerity, gentleness, modesty, consideration for others, and sunny nature made him a universal favorite. "A bright-eyed, vivacious, lovable lad of slender form, golden hair, ruddy complexion, winning ways; uncommonly mirthful, he was as fond of books as he was of fun,—" reported one of his early teachers.

Even as a child his sense of humor was displayed. A parishioner of his father in Charlestown told the writer that she recalled seeing the boy at church one

[6]

Sunday, sitting alone in the minister's pew. In the pew in front of him sat a woman with vividly red hair. Little Starr amused himself and his neighbors by repeatedly thrusting his finger at her fiery locks, and then quickly withdrawing it to blow upon it, with a comical simulation of agony on his roguish young face.

This mirthfulness was accompanied, however, by a deep sense of reverence. At table, we are told, when his father said grace, little Starr would fold his hands, close his eyes and bow his head, saying "Amen!" at the close—a habit he had not been taught but had himself adopted. He was faithful at church and Sunday School and seemed predestined for the ministerial calling, for which his gifts and inclinations, as well as the parental encouragement well fitted him. In his thirteenth year he had written a sermon, which was printed in a denominational paper.

The long illness and early death of Starr's father compelled him, however, to give up all thoughts of a college education, and the youth entered a store as clerk and bookkeeper, becoming at fifteen years of age the mainstay of his mother and the five younger children. Without murmur or complaint he accepted this disappointment of his hopes of a college education and professional career. One of his sisters, Angela Starr King (Moore)—be it said in passing— was a woman of brilliant parts, and later displayed rare gifts as a dramatic reader. Though now en-

[7]

gaged in business pursuits Starr King remained devoted to study and self-improvement. He formed a club with other like-minded young men for serious reading and discussion. He was an omnivorous and rapid reader of books, with a peculiar aptitude for philosophical study, reading metaphysical works with the ease and relish with which most young people devour novels. One of his teachers, Professor Tweed, says of him at this period: " He would read what seemed to me an involved and obscure passage from Kant—and when I began to express a doubt whether I perfectly understood it, he would instantly state it in terms which rendered it as clear as daylight. He was not a hard student; he was incapable of hard study. The most abstruse problems furnished him only with intellectual play. He had a natural affinity for knowledge. Its acquisition was not labor, but a delight." His correspondence with his friends on philosophical topics evinced a mastery of metaphysics, a power for generalizing and imparting the underlying principles of the differing schools of thought which would be remarkable in a mature scholar, much more so in a youth of eighteen. Attending the lecture courses on Natural Religion given by Rev. Professor James Walker of Harvard College at the Lowell Institute in Boston, he took notes in long hand of the whole series, and wrote out the twelve lectures of the third course in full. Three years later this reproduction was printed in a Boston newspaper. It was deemed an astonishing feat of mind and memory. He also attended the lectures of Professor Silliman on Chemistry, and other courses. The writings of Drs. W. E. Channing and James Martineau kindled within him sentiments of admiration and reverence, and profoundly affected his religious opinions. For Theodore Parker's school of thought and method of presentation he seems to have had less affinity. I can find no trace at this time of any noticeable influence of Emerson on his thinking. On Sundays he listened to the eloquent discourses of Rev. E. H. Chapin, who had succeeded his father in the Charlestown pulpit, and formed with that eminent divine a friendship which endured through life.

In the meantime his daily business duties were performed with conscientious care and to the entire satisfaction of his employer. He soon, however, exchanged these duties for the more congenial occupation of a school teacher; becoming at eighteen principal of a grammar school in Medford, Mass., whither the whole family removed in 1842. Here he not only found a larger field of labor and an enlarged income, but the rare good fortune of constant personal intercourse with the Universalist pastor of Medford, Rev. Hosea Ballou, 2nd, who later became the first president of Tufts College. Dr. Ballou was a learned scholar, and one of the most profound minds in the religious life of that day. This contact could not fail to be of great importance to Starr King's intellectual and religious development. He

[9]

gratefully spoke ever after of Dr. Ballou as his "theological father."

Theodore Parker, the great radical preacher of Boston, who met him in Medford at this time, records in his diary: "Saw Schoolmaster Thomas Starr King, capital fellow, only nineteen, has taught school three years, supports his mother, reads French, Spanish, Latin, Italian and a little Greek, and begins German. He is a good listener."

In 1843 Starr received the appointment of bookkeeper in the Charlestown Navy Yard, which not only increased his income but afforded more leisure for study. He was now deep in the German language and literature and found it a mine of intellectual riches. He always valued his descent, on the maternal side, from that student nation. An aunt, Miss Sarah E. Starr, only four years his senior, was a successful teacher of the German language and literature. A woman of poetic gifts and varied accomplishments she was highly esteemed by Starr King, as his correspondence with her discloses.

Hon. Richard Frothingham, of Charlestown, a near neighbor and intimate personal friend of Starr King, in a memoir of the latter published shortly after his death, gives much information concerning this period of Mr. King's life and reproduces some of his youthful correspondence with friends and fellow-students. He was now having "glorious times" in attending a philosophical class which met every Wednesday evening, and was reading Stewart on the philosophy of the mind. He read much, and sought rare books on this subject. When Dr. Ott's book on Hegel came out, he invited certain Harvard students to read it with him, and rich were the hours they had over this book. "I am at present," he wrote, "engaged in the study of a work on the latest school of German philosophy. It is by Dr. Ott, of Paris; and is an exposition of the system of Hegel. Kant's system is pretty difficult; but this ties the brain up in knots." He would attend at times in Boston German religious services on Sunday, in order to familiarize himself with the spoken language. Far into the night he would talk of Goethe and Schiller and their fellow-poets, and the German divines of the schools of Tholuck and De Wette. He read the works of Guizot and Schlegel on the philosophy of history. For Greek schools of thought he had an equal veneration, and would discourse for hours to a sympathetic listener on the greatness of a Socrates and a Plato. "Well do I remember," remarked his friend, Rev. A. D. Mayo, in an after-dinner speech in Faneuil Hall, "that the first day of our youthful acquaintance he read me into a fit of indigestion and a sleepless night with his Plato and Kant and Cousin; a night whose watchful hours I improved by maturing the resolution that on my return to my country home I would begin those philosophical studies in which he is second to no man of his age in our country." Mr. King, who was present on this occasion, in the course of a speech he made, wittily retorted:

"Let me say here, that however much interested I may have felt in philosophy generally, there is one system, verbally represented by one of the names just pronounced, which has done so much harm in the religious world that I try to get rid of it, and earnestly desire to see all pulpits and meetings utterly free from its poison—the system of *cant.*"

Among Starr's most intimate and beloved friends was Randolph Ryer of New York, a young man of similar tastes and aims, engaged, however, in business pursuits, with whom he corresponded for nearly twenty-five years. These letters may almost be considered a diary of his inner life. They abound in quips, banter, puns, and similar displays of his exuberant spirits and sense of humor. Whilst their private reading gives one a pleasant insight into the brilliant promise and lovable qualities of the writer and his capacity for friendship, they are, in many cases, of too personal and informal a character to permit extended quotation. Placed at our disposal we allow ourselves such extracts as throw light on his character and career.

In May, 1841, he tells his friend Ryer gleefully of a visit to O. S. Fowler, the phrenologist, who after the usual examination of the cranium, advises him to study law, as more in accord with his natural disposition because of his smallness of conscientiousness and veneration and the preponderance of combativeness and destructiveness, with large causality and hope! "On my asking him how I was qualified for

[12]

the ministry, he replied by laughing! telling me that this profession was out of the question, since I was by no means serious, and a lack of veneration would be a real defect." But, on insistence, Mr. Fowler said if he became a preacher his doctrine would be "thorough-going Universalism." He also prophesied that he would be a very eloquent speaker whatever profession he adopted, and would some day become an author.

In October, 1842, Starr asks the same friend: "How are politics in your quarter? Daniel Webster's speech made a stir in your village, I presume, as elsewhere. I had the happiness to listen to it as it rolled in burning tones from the 'God-like' lips. It was indeed powerful. That day I shall never forget. My bump of sublimity or idealism was pretty well fed. Webster in the morning and Edwin Forrest as Othello in the evening. Heavens! what a performance. I have seen that piece three times and could never tire of it. I think it is truly Forrest's masterpiece."

Starr was devoted to the drama, and went six times to hear Macready. Concerning Dr. Channing, whose recent death had created universal sorrow in liberal circles, he writes:

"Channing! All the eulogies that have been pronounced upon him throughout the land cannot do justice to him. The sermon of Dr. Bellows (many thanks for it) is a beautiful performance. I shall show it to Doctor Chapin. I dined with the last-

[13]

named on Sunday. He preached on last Sabbath afternoon. At the close Channing was mentioned in a touching and beautiful manner.

"Theodore Parker is lecturing here on 'The Times.' He is the immortal Parker. I send you a sermon of his on Channing. I went on Tuesday to a lecture on elocution by James E. Murdoch. Very fine."

He wrote long letters to the same friend on philosophical topics, explaining and summarizing the different schools of thought, ancient and modern, and advising him to read especially Cousin, Constant and Jouffroy. To do this profitably he should acquire a reading knowledge of French. "It will not take much time. In a few weeks you could read quite fluently."

In 1842 the youth of eighteen writes:

"I have been somewhat troubled of late by the perusal of a French work on the Eclecticism of Cousin and Jouffroy by Pierre Leroux. I had bid farewell to the last of the immortal dialogues of Plato, so poetic, so inspiring, so lofty, and then to change for a work of the nature of Leroux's was almost insupportable. The 'Refutation of Eclecticism' is a masterly performance, written in a burning yet logical style, occasionally beautified by a pounce upon Cousin personally, which is done, I assure you, in no very measured terms. In short the style is a capital exponent of one of Orestes Brownson's patent philosophers, all feeling and passion. In Leroux you can find the parentage of nearly all Brownson's new opinions. He acknowledges him, I think, as his spiritual Godfather. Well, I have finished the work, and am now employed in bringing the opposing gentlemen, Cousin and Leroux, to a reconciliation. Prejudice may account for much, but of all the writers whose thoughts I ever had the pleasure to become familiar with, whether for the style in which they are dressed or the clearness, with which they convey the truth, none delights as Victor Cousin."

In September, 1844, he writes:

"The current of my earthly existence flows gently and calmly. The inner man also is serene; resting trustfully in the arms of a glorious faith and a noble philosophy. Have you ever reflected on the intimate connection between revelation and philosophy, faith and reason? By many they are put in contrast, set in opposition. Yet they mutually explain and reciprocally aid each other. Faith in man implies the doctrine of the dignity of human nature. The doctrines of revelation must conform to the exhibitions which God has given us of his power, wisdom, glory, and goodness, through nature and the soul. Reason, instead of being subordinated to faith, is the very essence of faith, else faith is a blind idolatry. The true faith is the self-renunciation of reason where reason finds that it can know no farther. You, Randolph, take your faith directly from Christianity, and apply it directly to the condition of society. You desire the social manifestation of Christianity as the means of raising the individual. I also find that philosophy, as it is drawn from the crystallized instruction of nature, and from the mysterious depths of spiritual life, is confirmed and sanctified by Christianity. I look rather to the elevation of the individual as one great means of improving society. Both

[15]

tendencies are necessary. Neither should exclude the other. Eclecticism is the motto on the banner of the nineteenth century."

Not always was his mood as serene and cheerful as this. His soul had tasted of the bitterness of sorrow in the death of his father, the passing away of youthful and beloved friends, and the disappointment of his own cherished hopes. "The reality of loss," he wrote, "often oppresses me; exaggerated perhaps by the imagination, which always imparts an ideal hue to the experiences of the past as well as the expectations of the future. But," he continues, "I reverence the great law of compensation, even when it reveals itself to me in the distresses of the inner man."

Thus, in the companionship of books, by protracted, solitary studies, through daily contact with men and affairs, and the stern discipline of sorrow, self-denial and responsibility, this "graduate of the Charlestown Navy Yard," as he humorously described himself, acquired an education, and developed a character. It was not the best training for everybody, but it was doubtless sufficient for him, with his rare maturity of powers and balanced moral faculties. It is to be noted that in 1850 Harvard College admitted the adequacy of his preparation by conferring on Starr King the honorary degree of A.M.

CHAPTER II

IN THE MINISTRY

WITH his native gifts and early associations it was natural that Starr King should choose the Christian ministry as his permanent vocation. He took no regular course of theological training. He did not seem to require any. His early environment and courses of study, as well as his natural gifts, were an adequate preparation. He carefully trained his naturally rich and powerful voice under the best instructors, and this, with his fine artistic sensibilities, made him one of the most impressive and beautiful readers and speakers to whom it has ever been my privilege to listen. At the age of twenty he began to preach, Revs. Dr. Chapin and Theodore Parker both recommending him to parishes. His first sermon was delivered in Woburn, Mass. Later he occupied various pulpits in Boston and its suburbs, and also wrote for theological reviews, meanwhile performing his official duties at the Navy Yard with characteristic precision. His reports to his superiors were models. He had a natural aptitude for figures and wrote a singularly graceful and legible hand. In 1846, Dr. Chapin received and accepted a call to a Universalist church

[17]

in Boston. This left the Charlestown pulpit vacant, and the society immediately sought Thomas Starr King for their minister. After much hesitation he accepted, and in his twenty-second year was installed as pastor over the same Universalist parish to which his father had ministered. It was a delicate and difficult situation, but he proved equal to it, and his success as a preacher and pastor was immediate and gratifying. Two years later, however, he broke down with nervous exhaustion and sought restoration to health in a sea-voyage to the Azores. On his return, in October, 1844, he accepted a call—once before made and refused—to the Hollis Street Unitarian Church in Boston. This transfer to another denomination, while in accord with his own inclinations, caused no little feeling among his Universalist friends; although the theological differences between the two bodies are very slight, being mainly a matter of emphasis. The one lays stress on the fatherhood of God, the other on the innate worth of the human soul, or as Starr King himself wittily paraphrased it, "The one thinks God is too good to damn them forever, the other thinks *they* are too good to be damned forever," adding that the reason the two sects had not long since united was that they were really "too near of kin to be married."

The services at his installation as pastor of the Hollis Street Society, on December 6, 1848, were of unusual interest. Rev. N. L. Frothingham, of the First Church in Boston, offered the introductory

[18]

prayer; Dr. Hosea Ballou, 2nd, read the Scriptures; Dr. Orville Dewey of New York, whom he greatly admired as a preacher and man, delivered the sermon; Rev. William R. Alger brought the fellowship of the churches; Rev. Cyrus Bartol gave the charge to the new pastor; and Dr. E. H. Chapin the address to the people. These were all ministers of superior merit and station and his personal friends.

The Hollis Street Church was recognized to be a difficult post of duty, the temperance and anti-slavery issues which the former pastor, Rev. John Pierpont, introduced into the society by his drastic preaching having almost disrupted it. The new preacher had definite convictions on these subjects, but he also had tact, patience and a pedagogic training. Yet he did not hesitate to speak his mind on the topics of the hour, as the titles of some of his discourses in Boston indicate—"The Free Soil Movement," "The Fugitive Slave Law," and "The Dred Scott Decision." For eleven years he remained at Hollis Street Church, an earnest preacher, a widely admired, much beloved minister, and one of the most potent influences for good in the city.

On his twenty-fourth birthday, coincidently with his entry on his eleven years' pastorate at the Hollis Street Church, Starr King was married to Miss Julia Wiggin of East Boston, a woman of personal attractions, social gifts, and intellectuality. His home became the center of the gracious hospitality in which his soul delighted. While retaining his intimate relations with Drs. Ballou and Chapin, and other valued friends of his earlier life, he formed new ties with eminent thinkers and writers, such as Drs. Orville Dewey and Henry W. Bellows of New York, Dr. Cyrus Bartol, Dr. Frederick H. Hedge, Dr. Ezra S. Gannett, Revs. William R. Alger, Edward Everett Hale, Thomas B. Fox, and many of the laity. In the monthly meetings of the venerable Boston Association of ministers Thomas Starr King was an ever-welcome guest. No member contributed more to the life of the proceedings. Brought into close relations through his general culture and public lecturing with literary circles in Boston, in that day deemed the Athens of America, Mr. King found congenial companionship and appreciation among the authors and writers of New England. His amiability, wit and modesty, as well as his manifest abilities as a thinker and scholar, won their regard and affection.

Two theological controversies with orthodox opponents brought the young minister favorably before the religious public. One was a public discussion on "The Trinity" with Rev. F. H. Huntington, a prominent Unitarian divine and neighbor who had recently, and, as it was deemed by many, precipitately transferred himself to the ranks of the Episcopalian priesthood, and now sought to justify his changed ecclesiastical relations by what seemed an equally hasty and ill-considered defense of the traditional faith against the liberal school of opinion from which he had just seceded. Mr. King's discourses in reply, afterwards put into permanent form, were held to be masterpieces in argument, scholarship, fairness and courtesy, disclosing an aspect of his abilities which came as a surprise to many who had not realized the many-sidedness of the man.

The other controversy was with Dr. Nehemiah Adams, a leading orthodox divine of Boston, on the Doctrine of Eternal Punishment. Having listened to Dr. Adams on this subject, the young preacher invited him to repeat his discourse in the Hollis Street pulpit. This was done, and to an overflowing audience. The two discourses in which Mr. King replied to the unrelenting Calvinism of his adversary were greatly admired and deemed unanswerable.

As a pastor his devotion was unceasing, his quick and tender sympathy, his spiritual insight, tact, and unselfishness qualifying him rarely for the delicate and often difficult relation of a shepherd of souls. Meanwhile the poor, the distressed, the unfortunate, found in him a sympathizer, adviser and friend, a benefactor who gave not only of his means, but himself to their need. A more generous nature never breathed the air of New England.

Theodore Parker called Starr King the best preacher in Boston. It is certain that he had but one rival, and that was the radical preacher of the Music Hall himself. No clergyman was so much sought after socially. Wherever he went he was the life of the company, yet his popularity did not make

[21]

him self-conscious or self-satisfied. He was in very truth "The people's darling, yet unspoilt by praise."

From Starr King's unbroken correspondence with his friend Randolph Ryer we obtain an intimate acquaintance with the professional and personal life of the young minister at this period of his career. His letters disclose his thoughts and aims, his occupations and diversions, his admirations and friendships. They reveal the continual growth of his mind in range and insight, his increase in power of expression, and his consecration to his calling and his kind. We permit ourselves further extracts from them.

On April 2nd, 1849, he writes his friend:

"Since I wrote you last a project has been started for a large club to consist of free minds of all mental complexions and tendencies. Emerson, W. H. Channing, E. P. Whipple, John Weiss, John S. Dwight, James Freeman Clarke, etc., etc. are deeply interested in it, and I think we shall make it go, and make it a noble thing too. We intend to have a large room or set of rooms, with café under them, to procure gradually a library, to divide the club into different sections, ethical, scientific, poetic, religious, etc., and so have elaborate reports and discussions once a quarter. The preliminary meeting has been held, and was very fully attended. I was present. The next meeting will be a week from to-morrow. . . .

"Write and let me know what is going on in the world of Socialism. My friend Dana ought to have stayed in Europe a little longer; for the interests of harmonious humanity seem to be ajar since his powerful presence has been withdrawn. . . . Alcott comes to see me often, and we have gloriously muddy talks. He thinks I am a splendid fellow, and the way I pour mysticism into him is a caution. Two of his last orphic sayings were,—'I find that everywhere grandmother is a great myth.' 'My instincts always are authentic.' He thinks the Devil is the 'Almighty's flagellant' . . . I am in fine health and spirits."

To the same:

"June 4th, 1849.

"The noise and effervescence of Anniversary Week is over in this city. I attended quite a number of the meetings and by some of them was considerably refreshed. It was not my fortune, however, to listen to any great speeches or great speakers. I did not hear Wendell Phillips, nor Channing, nor Sumner, nor Parker. The most moving address I heard during the whole week was made by the black man who escaped from Richmond, Virginia, in a box five feet long, two wide, and two deep. It was simply told, but had an immense effect upon the whole audience. I thought while I listened to it, how much more powerful our Anti-Slavery societies would be if they would confine their efforts more to bringing such men and such cases before the community, and so try to make our northern conscience feel the barbarity of slavery, than they are by the methods of denunciation, virulent attacks upon the clergy and the Church, and desperate hostility to the Constitution and the Union. Let them direct all their efforts to exhibiting the curse of negro bondage and the ranks will soon be swelled by double the number of adherents which they possess at present. Why can't our reformers learn to have more confidence in *truth,* and less in human passion. I wish I could see a party once that felt they were the organs of immeasurable right, which, if they simply proclaimed it without heat, and violence, and personal allusion, would surely win. It is hard for a reformer to cultivate humility. It is not we that triumph by our eloquence and zeal. It is the *truth* which we state. It goes out on an impersonal mission, and when it has left our lips works by invisible and impersonal agencies. . . . A true reformer ought not to expect very speedy visible effects from the words he utters, and if his faith is religious, he will see that to publish his truth carelessly and with personal unconcern is the best method for his own peace and health of mind, and for the interests of righteousness among men."

It is interesting to contrast this earlier point of view concerning the proper function and method of the minister, with Mr. King's later course in California, in which as a preacher and popular orator he addressed himself so directly and effectively to the social sins and political misdoings which had plunged the nation into the great Civil War. Probably he still would have maintained that under normal social conditions the appeal to the individual reason and conscience, and man's general education in virtue and holiness, are the wisest methods for the religious teacher and reformer, but that in great crises of human society the circumstances and needs of the hour might demand a more drastic treatment, a direct attack upon specific evils in the social and political

[24]

order, the denunciation of the prophet as well as the pleading of the apostle.

Continuing this subject a week later he wrote his friend:

"I would insist as strongly as any one on the right and duty of ministers to act as reformers, to speak in Anti-Slavery meetings, and temperance and peace meetings, if they have the power of popular address. Let them act as Reformers in the proper sphere for such social action. And in the pulpit let them attack the central throne of sin in the private heart. If I prove to a man that his affections are inactive and cold, that he is not like Christ, and can inspire in his heart a sentiment of broad, comprehensive benevolence, am I not making him a Reformer? If I can make him loathe sin, and love right and goodness only, am I not leading him to hate slavery and drunkenness, which are only special forms of sin? If I expound to his intellect, and win his heart to feel the glory of the Christian relations of fellowship and brotherhood, am I not effectually aiding the cause of peace? If I lead him to recognize the divinity of self-sacrifice, am I not adding an instrument to all true reform agencies in Christendom? I think I am, and besides am making a true Christian in his heart, while many reformers only gain the aid of men's votes and hands to a Christian work, when the hearts of their allies may not be inwardly redeemed. This is my view of the work of the Church —to make men inwardly Christian by drawing out their affections to what is pure and holy, and thus sending them as reformatory agencies into society to work whichever way their active instincts move. . . . My church can't act as a Fourierite Committee, nor as an Anti-Slavery Society, but if I can send out through it good men and women with warm, Christion affections and strong religious wills I aid social reform in the highest way of which I am aware."

Certainly Starr King's conception of the pastoral office and mission of the preacher was an exalted one, and if ever a minister was equal to the moral miracle of transforming indifference into fervor, worldliness into character, and selfishness into service, Starr King was that man.

His next letter is of equal interest, treating of a problem in the work of the Liberal Christian minister which is still a subject of much discussion and pondering.

"September 10th, 1849.

"I exchanged yesterday with Mr. Lunt of Quincy, and while there, took tea with Charles Francis Adams at the old family mansion of John Adams and John Quincy Adams. Mr. Adams is quite a student of preaching and preachers, and I had a very instructive and pleasant conversation with him. His wife is perfectly rich in a *tête-à-tête*. He complained to me that Unitarian preaching is too cold, clear, rational and explanatory. It is too *moral,* and derives too little inspiration from the great religious principles of the New Testament. Everywhere among the cultivated I hear the same complaint. Is it not strange that a system of theology which was constructed to meet the wants of the intellect should so soon defeat the very purpose of its construction and cease to enlist the interest of the very faculty for which it was found necessary? The trouble is not

[26]

with the essential principles of the system, but with the preachers. We may keep all our philosophy, and yet preach with fervor.

"What intellectual conception is there so grand and elevating as that the Infinite Being, architect of Nature, artificer of suns and firmaments, *loves* humanity! . . .

"The need is not to go back to the mysteries of Orthodoxy, which paralyze and offend the intellect, but to proclaim more exclusively the great religious relations of the soul—the doctrine of God's paternity and our filial ties, and the spirit of self-sacrifice and disinterested goodness, which can wake the ashy life of the heart like a breeze fanning a coal to flame. These are the essential principles of Christianity: they separate it from philosophy: they will revive the world when the preachers come who can adequately proclaim them. Mrs. Adams thought the ministers ought to 'pepper' their sermons more with terrors, but her husband agreed with me."

His friend Ryer had been impressed with the writings of that brilliant but erratic genius, Orestes Brownson, whose conversion from extreme radical religious opinions and Socialistic experimentation to an ultra Roman Catholicism had created a sensation in the religious world. Starr King writes several times in confutation of this final outcome of Brownson's quest for truth.

"October 1, 1849.
"Have you seen the October no. of Brownson's Review? If not, get it. It will interest you especially because it contains a review of William Henry

[27]

Channing's general creed. The article is one of Brownson's strongest. It is a capital exercise of mind to read it. And the first article in it is also a poser. It is called: 'Protestantism in a Nutshell.' It is without exception the most impudent composition, probably, that ever saw the light. After exhausting every form of invective that a crazy fancy can invent, he brings the serious charge against Protestantism that it insults, and has always been hostile to, human reason; while the Catholic Church has always honored and employed it! Brownson ought to have a medal for his ground and lofty tumbling in the arena of logic.

"Of course you will go to hear Dr. Dewey on Wednesday evening. Write me how you like him. . . . The affairs of our society seem very promising and prosperous. But it is hard work to rebuild even in outward prosperity a broken parish. We had very good audiences yesterday, though the day was not pleasant. I preached two new sermons. One from the text: 'Nothing is secret that shall not be made manifest, neither anything hid that shall not be known and come abroad.' The subject was that all truth reveals itself. First, it is intended by the Almighty that all truth in the sphere of nature shall be known by the human intellect. It is hidden a little, so that our faculties are tasked to detect it, but not so hidden that earnest study cannot disclose it. Second, secret truths of character make themselves manifest. This is so in history. Men become known for what they are. A man that deserves fame gets it; and the kind of fame which he deserves he gets. The secrets of character reveal themselves unconsciously to those with whom we deal. Our looks often betray them. And the influence we exert, separate from our words, tells what we are. Third, all truth, even the minute secrets of the moral world, stands revealed to God. Fourth, the secrets of our lives will one day perhaps be terribly revealed to memory as a punishment. Fifth, the text may be a prophecy of the law of our being in another world. The secrets of character may there be known to each other, and this simple fact may furnish a portion of our reward, and the great portion of our punishment.

"In the afternoon the subject was: 'Thou art the man.'"

The two friends, in their correspondence, discussed the merits of Socialism as a creed for the conduct of life. Ryer was much inclined to it; King, though ever preserving an open mind, was less so.

To the same:

"November 5, 1849.

"Perhaps you will consider it an era in my life that I met Henry James (Senior) last Thursday evening at the Association's Rooms on High Street, and heard him read an essay on Socialism. I was delighted to meet him. We talked some together. I like him as a man. But his essay was irrational, though very able. He denied that there is any such thing as sin, said that no law of God could be violated, and that the fact of a violation would prove that it was no divine law. The doctrine of free agency he considered puerile and contemptible. Yet he blowed up the existing arrangements of society unmercifully, and showed that they were false in every respect. Now I could not help audaciously querying to myself, how it is that God's laws of *society* could be violated any more than His other laws, and why the fact that Socialism is not triumphant does not prove, according to Mr. James' theory, that it must be false. If no law of God can be violated, then whatever *is* is right; Society with its false constitution *is,* therefore it is right. From this logical dilemma Mr. James cannot save his essay."

To the same:

"November, 1849.

"I preach at times, and perhaps shall preach more freely in future on social aspects and needs. On Fast Day I shall speak on 'The Lights and Shadows of our Age.' Next Sunday afternoon I shall give a lecture on Paul, the first of two. But I must respect the intimations of the spirit in my natural conformation, and preach generally from the spontaneous insights afforded me into the truths of the Gospel.

"Yesterday morning I preached a sermon on Old Age. Three very old and most exemplary Christians have recently died here who were connected with our parish, and I was moved to notice it in that way. I took up the point that Old Age is a period of Revelation, when the intrinsic repulsiveness and evil of sin is more clearly revealed than in any other stage of life, and when the glory and worth of religious principles and graces seem most powerfully portrayed. If we would know what profanity, avarice, epicureanism, bad temper, etc. are, we must study them in an *old* sinner, when they have inwrought themselves thoroughly with the character, and are unrelieved by any accidental graces and neu-

[30]

tral qualities. If we would see the power and peace imparted by Christian faith and practice, and observe the Christian graces in their holiest attire, we must study them in an *old* saint in whom they transfigure the wrinkles, and beautify the tottering steps, and throw a halo about the bleaching hair.

"Just think of an atheistic childhood and an infidel old age and the shock given to our sympathies and finest sensibilities proclaim that human nature is wronged by such an hypothesis, its beauty soiled, its proper symmetry broken.

"After dwelling upon the sanctity which Christianity has imparted to old age, the sermon treated fully of the adaptation of Christian principles and promises to the special needs of the aged, and how weak and miserable an old person, in whom the best feelings are not withered, would be without their support. The discourse was closed with a picture of the glory of old age as the Bible reveals it in the aged saints its pages portray—Abraham, Moses on Mount Pisgah, Samuel in the decline of life, David waking the penitential tremors of his harp with failing fingers, Simeon in the temple, John the Apostle when a hundred years old, Paul the aged ready to be offered after the good fight of faith.

"Last night Julia and I went to hear the oratorio of the Creation for the second time this season. It was only second to the original Creation by the Omnipotent. I think it is the richest piece of music one can hear. Its waves of melody roll over the spirit like floods of ethereal joy from the New Jerusalem. I grow more and more impressible to music. A few years ago it was a blank to me. Now a sixth sense is opened."

After a long and serious illness Mr. King wrote his friend:

"February, 1850.

"I am quite well again with the exception of a little hoarseness. I lecture to-night in Methuen, talk in the Bible-Class an hour to-morrow night, address the Mercantile Library Association Wednesday evening, and lecture in Brookline on Thursday. Yesterday I preached three times—in the afternoon on 'Samson, or Waste of Powers.' I like it better than any sermon I ever wrote.

"Next week I am to be engaged in preparing a sermon on 'Life, a Trust, a Discipline, an Achievement,' to be preached on Sunday evening as one of a course in the Bedford Street Church. I shall try to make it the best I ever wrote, for certainly the subject is magnificent. In the morning I am to preach before the students and professors of Harvard College—a trying service."

To the same:

"April 1, 1850.

"I have just left the Supreme Court Room, and heard what I never heard before, the sentence of death pronounced on a prisoner. Chief Justice Shaw completed the terrible drama that has thrilled every one here for the last few weeks, by the solemn words of judgment upon Professor Webster. I cannot say anything in relation to it. It was awful in the extreme. God save him, for his family's sake, from the scaffold! Yesterday morning I preached in the college chapel at Cambridge, where Professor Webster attended church. It wrung my nerves beyond anything I ever experienced in the pulpit."

[32]

IN THE MINISTRY

On his return from his summer vacation at the end of July, 1850, spent among his beloved White Mountains and at Rockland, by the sea, he writes to the companion of his journeys:

"I presume you got home safely.   But how do you bear business again?   For myself, I am homesick already, and long to be again among the mountain peaks.   Isn't your mind also stored with rich images of Lake Winnepiseogee and Red Hill, and North Conway, with Mt. Kearsarge, and the ride to Old Crawford's and the Willey House and Mt. Willard, and Tom the Mountaineer that saw the Transfiguration, and caught a deer by the horns and opened its jugular vein with a penknife!   And Mt. Washington and the gullies, the Old Man of the Mountains, and Echo Lake, and the bath in the Pemigewasset, and that divine walk, and the basin where that poor stick still waltzes round, and the Flume!   O Randolph, shall we ever have another such walk as that?   I fear not this side of Jordan.   There must be grand mountain scenery in Heaven.   I hope we shall see it together—if I am found worthy.   In my musings it seems as if North Conway might be the entrance gate to Paradise. . . . You know, I presume, that I am now an A.M., by the grace of Harvard College. Only think of it.   Wonder when I shall be P.M. Probably not till after the meridian of life."

Mr. King was exquisitely sensitive to Beauty in all its forms, particularly so to the art of music, which had not disclosed its full charm and delight to him until this stage of his development.   In October, 1850, he writes his soul-friend:

[33]

"I have heard Jenny Lind. Five times in all I have listened to the inspired Swede, thanks to her manager P. T. Barnum's kindness. What shall I say of her singing? She put her voice underneath the vast audience and fairly lifted them up on its sea-like swells, and tossed them like toys upon the crests and sparkling foam of her warbles and trills and ornaments. The whole orchestra accompaniment at times was as nothing to her flood of easy, revelling melody, and it seemed as if the stars must be moved at last to pipe out again in chorus, and all the sons of God shout for joy. . . . I have never before appreciated music, never conceived the glory and sweetness of the human voice, never understood the capacity of music to bear the burden of great sentiments, and interpret, by a cadence or a single note, a truth as broad as the universe and deep as the soul."

To the same:

"October 29, 1850.

"I preached in Concord on Sunday. The great Transcendentalist, Ralph W. Emerson was at church in the afternoon. In the evening I took tea in company with him and passed a portion of yesterday morning in his study. I enjoyed seeing him, as always, and on some points we had a good talk. He belongs in the same cabinet of Nature's Jewels with Plato and Jenny Lind. Plato the ruby, Emerson the white, cold, flashing diamond, Jenny Lind the pearl. . . . I shall commence writing my lecture on Socrates this week."

Filling an important pastorate in a great city, the young minister was daily brought into contact with the moral and social problems of urban life, and the responsibility of the more favored and privileged classes to ameliorate the evils, and equalize the conditions of the existing order of society.

"April 28, 1851.

"A splendid present, my friend, those volumes of Fourier! I delight to look at them. The first leisure day or two I have shall be thoroughly pledged to Fourier, and I will make faithful report to you. As yet, you know, I have not read a line of his writings.

"What a day's work I had yesterday! Spoke to the Sunday School in the morning, preached a long Easter sermon, delivered a lecture of an hour and a quarter in the afternoon on Paul as a writer, and made an address in the evening at the Warren Street Chapel of nearly half an hour. You would have been satisfied with the dispensation yesterday, I think, for in the morning I gave the people Christianized Science, and in the evening Christianized Socialism. The sensual objections to the idea of immortality was the theme in the forenoon, . . . a glorious meeting we had in the evening. It would have filled your soul, and given you a foretaste of the millenium. Robert C. Winthrop presided, and made a most elegant and noble speech. It was Christian duty set to music. I moved the adoption of the Report of the doings of the Chapel for the past year. Let me give you one passage from the speech, of which I wrote the heads before I went. The time has come when, as a Christian community, we must either openly reject, or ingrain with our conscience, the truth—'we that are strong ought to bear the infirmities of the weak, and not to please ourselves, for Christ pleased not himself.' Not only in His word does God call

[35]

on us to obey this law, but also by unveiling to us, as in fiery hieroglyphics, the visible necessity of obeying it. The question of absorbing interest to society itself is this—how shall the Church, which contains the regenerative principles of truth, be brought from its serene and comfortable elevation into redeeming contact with the streets, lanes, and cellars of the world, with the Pariah caste of society in our modern cities, with the uncivilizing elements of our civilization, with this wide chaos of irresponsible and neglected vice, that lies outside our order and threatens to engulf it. The question is shall our light encroach upon the shadows and dispel them, or shall the shadows absorb the light? If we will not take up this problem of pauperism and ignorance in the large spirit of Christian duty and love, and consider, through some constructive methods the *rights* of the poor, it will be pressed upon our self-interest as involving the existence, or at least the health of society. God is showing us, by uncovering the horrors in our large centres of civilization, and the effects they are producing upon our welfare, that in the very warp of the social fabric is woven the law—'Whether one member suffer all the members suffer with it.' . . . Directly those classes cannot get the life, truth, hopes and life of the Gospel. It must go from us, the more favored, who have our hands upon the great electric force, and by touching *them,* convey to them its blessed and enlivening stream. Especially in this country, with our theory of the State, should we earnestly consider this social problem. Our lower classes clutch the ballot-box, and we are indissolubly united with them in our interests and our life. They are every way bone of our bone. Our highest classes, like the apex of a pyramid, are lifted up from the broader base gradually widening below. What hope is there for us, if that base is rotting at its lowest tier, or slumping in a moral marsh? Will the pyramid stand with such insecurity of foundation, with such chemistry gnawing the bottom of its structure? It is safer, in our land, to have atheistic scholars than an atheistic, barbarous people; as it is safer for any frame to have diseased or blinded eyes than a canker spot on the heart."

Mr. King's letters during these early years of his Boston ministry disclose the new gained happiness of his wedded and home life and the brighter aspects of his residence in Boston. Their summer vacations were spent at the seaside and the mountains.

"PIGEON COVE, August 19, 1851.

"Would you could know the perfect accord here of the country and the sea. Rev. Mr. Bartol and family are here as usual, so that delightful and elevating companionship completes the circle of rich and reviving influences. We do a little reading. De Quincey's new book, 'Life and Manners,' Ruskin's 'Seven Lamps of Architecture,' a fine book on Paul's Letters to the Corinthians by Rev. J. H. Thom of Liverpool, some reviews, and an excellent volume called 'Companions of My Solitude,' by an English lawyer, make up my stock of literary exercises."

The following summer, 1852, he is again at Cape Ann, where in subsequent years a portion of his vacation season was almost invariably spent.

"It is glorious here. Would you could see our horizon line of ocean and take a promenade with us

[37]

in the woods. Our church is closed for four Sundays
and I have entire rest. Mr. Bartol is with us, serene
and mellifluous as ever. He preached gloriously last
Sunday. I hold forth to-day. Chapin is here and
is boiling over with fun, recasting language in all
shapes of pun-gency."

Writing in September following he tells of preaching two sermons on the recent Railway Jubilee in
Boston, discourses which were printed and rapidly
taken. Theodore Parker, whose own church services were suspended because of repairs in the edifice,
was present at both the morning and evening services.

In January, 1852, his first child, Edith, was born,
an occasion that brought great joy to the household.
His friend Ryer also was happily married, and the
two friends exchanged their congratulations and kind
wishes.

"March 5th, 1852.

"Last week was another season of hard work.
Lectured on Monday night at Dorchester, Tuesday
in New Bedford, Wednesday in my vestry, Thursday at Salem, Friday at Newburyport, and on Saturday went to hear the Oratorio of St. Paul, one of the
greatest of Mendelssohn's compositions. One lives
an age during the two hours and a half that such
music sweeps the strings of the soul. I was so ill
that I could hardly hold up my head when I went
to the Concert, but sat through the whole, though it
was the third time I had heard it this season. I was
hardly strong enough to preach yesterday, having a
cold on all the nerves, but got through the two services of the day."

[38]

"April 12th, 1852.

"Last week I wrote two sermons, one for Fast Day on Public Sentiment, in which I opened distinctly on slavery, much to the delight of Rev. Dr. Francis, head of the Cambridge Divinity School, who was present and said, 'God bless you for that discourse!'"

A warm admirer of the philosophic thinker, James Martineau of England, Mr. King, in 1852, edited a volume of selected essays by his pen under the title "Miscellanies," the first American reprint of any of his writings. He also collaborated with his friend William Rounseville Alger in the republication of other of his books.

Efforts were made to induce the young minister to accept the vacant Unitarian pulpit in Brooklyn, New York. Born in the latter city, Mr. King always had a strong affection for it, and by repeated visits had made many friends and become as well known in the great metropolis of American life as in Boston itself. In January, 1853, he writes:

"As to church matters—poor Brooklyn! Unfortunate Chauncy Place! Happy Hollis Street! It is all settled. Last night capped the climax. The people at Hollis Street won't listen to my going. More than forty pews have been sold, our debt has been paid. We shall have funds over. They raise my salary to $3000, and will build a new and handsome pulpit and otherwise improve the church. This will stop my miscellaneous lecturing, except when the fee is $50. Isn't that doing bravely? I

[39]

shall stay. Yet my heart yearns towards Brooklyn. If I could I should have gone to them."

"March 14, 1853.

"We were quite disappointed, I assure you, that your letter only and not yourself arrived on Saturday. Little Petty was not reconciled to the arrangement. She could not read the epistle, but she could have had a good time with you and had made up her mind for a grand frolic. She never has been so good and cunning as yesterday, partly because it was her birthday (13 months old), and partly because she expected you and meant to have a jubilee. You must come this week or her little nerves won't stand the shock. . . . Bless her delicious heart! She's playing on my study floor, now while I write, and chirping with delight as sweetly as the spring birds sang by our own windows yesterday morning—forty of them in a row—the first gush of spring!"

His love of music and the drama continued to provide him with opportunities for relaxation and artistic enjoyment which did much to ease the strain of his professional life.

"May 2nd, 1853.

"I have been engaged in opera-ting. Not in stocks but on benches in the Howard Athenaeum. Madame Sontag's opera troupe is in Boston. Some kind friend has sent us tickets thus far for every performance, and I have attended six times, four times with Julia. It has been a great treat. We have never had an opera troupe that has done everything so well, that has given us such a complete artistic whole, and finished off the minor effects, such as dress,

[40]

position, scenery, chorus and subordinate parts so elaborately. And then Madame Sontag's voice, so clear, so bright, so cheerful, so perfectly cultivated, is like a sheaf of sun-rays, fluted and nodding with Corinthian luxury and grace. O that I understood music as a science! It is the most subtle and mighty vehicle of expression, and perhaps is the rudiment of the speech through which our souls are to gain and utter wisdom in the world to come."

"March 28, 1853.

"Preached twice in the Harvard College Chapel yesterday. I didn't enjoy it at all. Dined with Dr. Walker, president of the college, and had a glorious nooning with him. He never heard me in the pulpit before and said that I preached better than he had expected. . . . I am to lecture before the Benevolent Fraternity of Churches on behalf of the Ministry at Large. Last Saturday night the Germanians gave a superb concert, the best of the season. A Portland paper recently made an attack on my style of lecturing, which drew out a beautiful reply from an artist of that city, very complimentary."

In a more serious vein he writes his friend, on entering the thirtieth year of his life:

"January 1st, 1854.

"How ominous that figure (1854) looks! We are fast getting to be old fogies, Randolph. Fourteen years since we first met! What changes, what growths of mind, what slippings away from old moorings, what scootings out from narrow circumstances and little lakes of experience into wider bays, towards the great sea! Little did I imagine, fourteen

[41]

years ago, that I should ever have such a position of trust in the world as Providence has gently lifted me up to, by the easiest inclined plane of continuous accident. But here I am, a little wiser than then, with some serious purpose, I believe, hidden somewhere in my bosom, with some little gratitude, I trust, towards Providence that has done for me so much better than I deserve, and with a love for a few old friends which I hope the year 1874, if it sees me here, will find only riper, and which, I pray, may be perfected, if we shall then have passed on.

"You, Randolph, always believed that I would come to something, when I did not dream that I had the capacity for adorning any pedestal. Your attachment has been a great comfort to me; your friendship has been pure enough to be accounted a choice privilege in any life. Your household and William C——'s belong to the selected circle around the fireside of my heart. God bless you with a happy New Year!

"As to presents. Such a New Year's present as I have had! Champney's great picture of the White Mountains! And who could send me such a princely gift but that glorious Mr. Thaxter. He made the church a New Year's gift of a christening font of marble. Exquisite. You have no idea how superbly our church looks now (since extensive improvements)."

To the same:

"February 13, 1854.

"Pet is two years old to-day. How much enjoyment we have had with her these two short years! People talk of the indebtedness of children to parents, our debt is the other way. Pet has done more for us

[42]

than we for her. There is great beauty in the old prophecy of the triumph of righteousness on the earth—'and a little child shall lead them.' It tells of a time when domestic life shall be the brightest, and the joy and wisdom of mature natures shall flow from the training of childhood.

"Last evening I spent with Bayard Taylor at E. P. Whipple's. Bayard came to hear me preach yesterday morning, and said he was glad once to hear a sermon that he could agree with. We had a glorious time last evening talking of the Himalayas, the desert, the Nile, Etna, Gibraltar and the Arabs. He is delightful."

To the same:

"March 19, 1854.

"This morning I preached on Liberal Christianity as a positive faith, showing that all the positive elements which can belong to a religion are in ours, if preachers only have vitality enough to make them glow. It produced quite an impression on our people. O that we might wake them up to a feeling of the rich elements our faith contains, so that this weak, compromising twaddle would be banished from the pulpit and press. Dr. Orville Dewey is to preach in our church this evening before the Young Men's Christian Union. I had a very pleasant talk with him yesterday. He is noble and sound in religious thought. I like his views and Martineau's better than those of any living men I know. I see light ahead—am almost out of the thicket of lectures. Two more and I am free.

"P. S. I am just come from hearing Dr. Dewey. It was grand. He is a sentimental Webster. His

[43]

subject was the Worth of Virtue. It was comprehensive, practical, poetical, tender and majestic. It took hold of me. Preaching is the great business."

Starr King was not among the foremost of Anti-Slavery agitators. His youth and gentleness of nature, as well as his views on the methods and mission of the ministry precluded this, yet how deeply his sympathies were enlisted on this side, and what admirable service he rendered is shown by the following letter:

"June 12, 1854.

"I didn't write you last Monday, for I was used up after the great week of excitement in anniversaries and fugitive-slaveism.

"The slave excitement here was intense. I never knew such a stirring up, such inward gnashing of teeth. We were under martial law on Friday, and it turns out illegally so, and if anybody had been shot by the troops, the soldiers would have been liable for murder. The indignation is very deep against the mayor, and that poor Burns, by marching down State Street at noon under military guard, made more Abolitionists than Parker and Phillips have made in a year.

"The Sunday after the slave capture the churches were vocal with strong preaching. Hunkers were in great distress, having no rest for the soles of their feet. I preached on the arrest, trial and condemnation of Jesus, and the features of it as a judicial process which have made it infamous in after times. It made a great stir. The features of the trial correspond most wonderfully to that of poor Burns. The character of the evidence on which Jesus was con-

[44]

demned, the manner of his arrest, the unsuccessful attempt at rescue, the conspiracy of the two sets of officers—the city authorities of Jerusalem, and Pilate, the commissioner of Rome, the Court Room filled with brutal scamps, the efforts to release Jesus, and the refusal because Caesar would be offended, the Condemnation, which in Jerusalem was on Friday morning, at 9 o'clock (just the same as in Boston) the military escort to the place of execution, the giving of a new robe to Jesus (here they gave Burns a new suit before he left), and the triumph of the new religion because of that brutal show in the Passover Anniversary Week in Jerusalem—made a picture that delighted the majority of the parish and quite enraged the Hunker brethren. Some threatened to leave, etc., but they were all out yesterday, and I guess I shall triumph."

A pleasant picture of Mr. King's friendships and literary pre-occupations at this period is given in a letter to Rev. William Rounseville Alger, the author-divine of Boston.

"PIGEON COVE, ROCKPORT,
"August 1, 1854.

"My Dear Alger:
"I meant to write you, in reply to your kind and welcome note, before I left here for Down East, but procrastinated and failed. I have just returned. Loammi Ware was ordained last Wednesday. I took part. Dr. Bellows was there, preached only *so so,* but personally, spherically, conversationally, was glorious. We had a rich time together. Somehow we fit handsomely. His railroad talk, going down, was brilliant and inspiring to a degree I have

[45]

never known equalled. About Robert Schuyler, who was his parishioner, he monologued as wonderfully as De Quincey. Ware has a difficult post. Sylvester Judd's daguerreotype is in every heart in Augusta, and the spirit of his thoughts in all their souls.

"After leaving Augusta I went to the White Mountains and Dixville Notch with James T. Fields. The weather was splendid and we had an unsurpassable time. I want once to take you on the Eastern side and taste the scenery, mesmerically, through your delight. We must do it another season.

"On the way I read Thoreau's 'Walden' in an advance copy. The first half disappointed me as being poorer than 'Concord and Merrimac.' But the latter half is wonderful; the chapter on 'Spring,' 'Winter Animals,' with a description of squirrels, the 'Conclusion' being more weird and winding farther into the awful vitalities of nature than any writing I have yet seen. I envy you your approaching rapture. Alas, I left my copy in the cars. I have read Hurlburt's 'Gan Eden,' on Cuba; it is written with honey instead of ink."

In the spring of 1855 we hear for the first time of a literary project. "Would that I could study more and write less! I am at work on a book to interpret the landscape of the White Hills." He tells us also:

"I have been looking into spirit rappings again, somewhat. The spectres seem to be more powerful than they were. Some of the developments are really wonderful. Such antics as I have seen with pianos and tables! Hard to account for except on the theory of an outskirt of imps let loose over the border of the spiritual world."

Later experiences made him sceptical of any spiritual content in such "manifestations." As a member of a committee of investigation, headed by Professor Agassiz and other scientists, he became disillusionized. When one medium, who caused lurid written messages to appear on his arm, was found to have employed phosphorus in their production, Starr King ruefully remarked, "It only resulted in 'fuss-for-us.'"

The unveiling of the Benjamin Franklin statue in Boston, his birthplace, September 14, 1856, on which occasion Dr. E. H. Chapin delivered an oration, was followed by a supper at Starr King's house with Chapin, E. P. Whipple, James T. Fields, and Daniel Haskell, editor of the *Boston Transcript,* among the guests. We can image the cheer and wit of the occasion. This was only one of a long succession of such hospitalities. In November, 1857, Mr. King invited a company of his friends to meet Charles Mackay, the English reformer and poet, at a breakfast. Drs. Bellows, Hedge and Bartol, Whipple, James T. Fields, George Sumner, talented brother of the statesman Charles Sumner, William R. Alger and William B. Green were among the guests. "It was a brilliant three hours," writes Starr King.

Starr King's public attitude on the subject of Anti-Slavery became more and more pronounced. Thus

[47]

at the opening of a series of lectures on slavery delivered in Boston in the winter of 1856 he read—with what effectiveness we can imagine—Whittier's somewhat lengthy poem "The Panorama," a powerful arraignment of both the Northern and Southern States for their course with regard to the national sin of slavery.

To his friend Ryer he writes:

"April 4, 1857.

"Boston is in full bloom intellectually. Whipple is lecturing twice a week on the literary men of Shakespeare's time. They are marvellous lectures. I attend them all, and feel that is a great privilege. Emerson also lectures on Wednesday evenings. I go to them also. They are very interesting, but not up to his tide-line. Beecher is to be here. Tuesday night he will trot out the ghost of Burns. Thursday night Winthrop lectures. And we have been enjoying great music. Moreover, I am working hard on my White Mountain book. It is well along. They want me to settle in Chicago and offer a new church and $5000 salary. I seriously think of going."

CHAPTER III

MR. KING'S talents soon called him into the lecture field. It was the era of the Lyceum system, that great lecture campaign which preceded the Civil War, and afforded the best writers and speakers an opportunity to discuss before audiences of the most thoughtful and earnest people the great moral and social topics of the day. It was natural that Starr King should be attracted to this enlargement of his sphere of influence. As he told his Boston congregation: "The lecture offers a noble medium of influence. Many of the gifted men who pour their power through that channel speak from a consecration as manifest as the best preaching betrays. I cannot regret that I have been drawn so widely into that field, for it has been simply a necessity." The inadequacy of the salary which the church was able to pay Mr. King compelled him to add to his resources by lecture engagements. One third of his income from the Hollis Street Society he devoted to his mother and a brother incurably ill. He speedily became very popular on the lecture platform and extended his real parish from Boston all the way north to Bangor, and west to Chicago

[49]

and St. Louis. Yet his earnings from this source were small, as compared with the fees received nowadays by lecturers of equal rank. From ten to twenty-five dollars was considered a sufficient remuneration for a lecture in New England, and fifty dollars if delivered at the West. It is probable, Mr. Whipple tells us, that Mr. King's income was not increased over fifteen hundred dollars a year by his lecture engagements; while their drain on his physical and nervous vitality was tremendous. Mr. King's lectures, like those of many of his contemporaries, were largely sermons extended and popularized for Lyceum use. They dealt with the ethical and social life, and were designed to upbuild the spiritual side of man's nature, to strengthen faith in the true, the beautiful and the good as the chief and permanent interests of the human soul.

It is noteworthy that Starr King selected as the topic of his first lecture the great and many-sided German writer Goethe, of whose life and works he had made a close study. It was much admired. Dr. James Walker, the scholarly president of Harvard College, said that it was not merely remarkable that so young a man should have delivered such a lecture, but that any man could have given it. It was but the prelude to an output of brilliant and popular utterances on the lecture platform which soon placed Thomas Starr King in the very front rank of lyceum orators, and made him widely known and admired throughout the United States as a clear and forcible

thinker, a gifted rhetorician, and a persuasive advo-
cate of the higher interests of American life and
letters. He was ranked as one of the four great
luminaries of the lecture platform, the others by general consent being Wendell Phillips, Dr. E. H.
Chapin and Henry Ward Beecher. Starr King was
the youngest of this quartette of orators, and held
his own by gifts different from the others yet none
the less fascinating and meritorious. As Dr. Henry
W. Bellows tells us: "Starr King was more versa-
tile, more scholarly, more artistic than they. His
lectures were more balanced, finished and ornate.
His keen analytic sense and philosophic acumen gave
to his addresses an intellectual basis and breadth often
wanting in those of his great rivals," who, be it said
in passing, were also amongst his warmest friends
and dearest companions. "His keen intellect caught
at the laws immersed in bewildering details. He delighted to link together the most opposite and incongruous things; by some subtle association of thought
to give a local habitation and a name, a costume and
a character to the vague notions, ideas, fancies and
impressions floating in men's brains." Of such a
nature, as their very title indicates, were his famous
lectures: "Substance and Show;" "Sights and Insights;" "The Ideal and the Real;" "Existence and
Life." To this subtlety and analytic power was
added an acquaintance with the latest developments
of scientific thought, making his lectures brilliant
summaries of the latest philosophy illustrated by the

newest scientific disclosures. The gorgeousness of his rhetorical imagination, the incessant play of his humor and the electric character of his delivery, all contributed to make him the idol of the lecture platform.

On January 29th, 1849, Starr King writes his friend Randolph Ryer:

"January 29th, 1849.
". . . The first of the week I was engaged in retouching my lecture (before the Mercantile Library Association) on History. I improved it, in my judgment, considerably. Such a house you never saw. It was jammed and crammed, the largest of the season, except when Webster spoke. Every seat was filled, two hundred extra ones were provided, and then at least a hundred people stood around the doors. It took with critics and people, the audience were amazingly still, except when they applauded, which was not seldom.

"Emerson gave us last Monday evening the most brilliant lecture I ever listened to from any mortal. It was on the identity of the laws of the mind with the laws of nature. . . . To-night he lectures again. I fear I may lose it."

A lecture on Socrates was especially dear to Mr. King, and did much to introduce the ancient Greek philosopher and his era to the plain men and women who made up the bulk of the Lyceum audiences. It is even now a readable and delightful paper, and should lead to the study of the great thinker and moralist of classic antiquity. Mr. Whittier related

[52]

that he once loaned a volume of Socrates' great disciple Plato to a Yankee farmer of his acquaintance. He returned the book after an interval. "How did you enjoy my friend Plato?" asked the poet. "I liked him fust-rate," was the answer. "I see he's got hold of some of my idees." So Mr. King's lectures "domesticated" Socrates in the towns and cities of the East and West, making his audiences feel that they had a natural affinity with what was best and most inspiring in the thinking and life of classic antiquity.

For Daniel Webster's intellectual and rhetorical powers Mr. King had an unbounded admiration. He was among the first to appreciate the contribution which that great orator and writer had made to American literature as well as politics. He paid eloquent tribute to the eminent public service which Mr. Webster had rendered as an expounder of the American Constitution, and defender of the National idea against sectional aggression and party rancor. Mr. King's lecture on "Webster and the Constitution," delivered with especial frequency and fervor during the era of the Civil War, reveals one of the chief sources of his own patriotic inspiration and political sagacity.

August, 1852, finds him at work on an oration for Waterville College, Maine. Its topic was "Property." It was in reality a sermon expanded for the present purpose—more than half being entirely new.

" I didn't pay much respect to the sensual and hard-fisted estimates of goods and possessions, and I closed with an appeal to the young men to be prophets of the intellect and do something to reduce the American scepticism in the reality of all things which their hands could not grasp, and the Yankee limitation of beauty to the yellow hue of gold.

"It was delivered to an audience more densely packed than I ever saw before, and was well received. The society professed themselves satisfied. The Baptists were quite liberal, and I came home encouraged for the prospects of liberal Christianity among the rising generation of Evangelicals. Beecher has many young sympathizers that back him up. My production will not be printed, nor will my recent 4th of July oration before the Boston City authorities. I have declined the honor." [1]

To *Randolph Ryer:*

"November 8, 1850.

"Socrates is finished in the first draft. I have yet to copy it, and recast it, in a measure, for delivery in Lyceum courses. At present all the materials I have collected would consume two hours in the reading. Last Thursday night I delivered it at Quincy. It was liked, I am told, but I was satisfied that it needs a great deal of pruning to fit it for public success."

"November 24, 1850.

"On Sunday afternoon I lectured on the religious views of Socrates. We had a splendid congregation to hear it. I believe people generally were aston-

---

[1] It was put into print thirty-two years later, in 1884, by the authorities of the City of Boston.

ished to find what noble and spiritual views of God, duty, the soul, providence and prayer Socrates entertained. On Thanksgiving day I shall preach on the Nineteenth Century and the Progress and Prospects of Humanity."

"October 11, 1852.

"My amanuensis was laid up with weak eyes last week and I was compelled to write a sermon myself. It was hard work for me. I am going into New York State in January to six or seven principal places. Shall stop a Sunday at Niagara Falls."

A month later he preaches a sermon on the death of Daniel Webster, and writes:

"I am driven with rewriting Lyceum lectures, writing sermons and preparing the discourse on Webster for the printing. The church was full to hear it, though the Sunday was stormy. Thanks for Bellows' sermon. It was very characteristic, rich, poetic, bold and noble. I enjoyed reading it more than any other. With regard to Webster's 7th of March speech, I simply put two hypotheses as to Webster's motives. If he acted from political expediency and ambition he fell; if from broad views of permanent comprehensive benefit to all races, in the long run, by preserving the Constitution and the Union (which I prefer to believe) his action was, to himself, conscientious and heroic. I can't read his heart and therefore couldn't take the responsibility of deciding further."

Concerning his lecture, "The Laws of Disorder," Wendell Phillips told me a story which illustrates Mr. King's resourcefulness and tact. Mr. Phillips

[55]

had been invited to lecture in a New Hampshire town
—I think it was Manchester—and asked to name
his fee. As was his habit he replied, "If my topic
may be Anti-Slavery I will come for nothing and pay
my own expenses. If "The Lost Arts" or any other
of my literary addresses is demanded I shall have to
lecture for F. A. M. E.; as Dr. Chapin has put it;
that is 'Fifty-And-My-Expenses'!" It was finally
arranged that Mr. Phillips should speak in their Lyceum Course on "The Lost Arts," and later in the
evening, as was his frequent custom, address those
who might desire to remain and hear him on Anti-
Slavery. This program was carried out, but gave
great offense to the pro-slavery element among the
subscribers. The succeeding lecturer in the course
was Thomas Starr King. Before introducing him
to the audience the chairman sought to allay the feeling which had been created the week previous. "I
regret," he began, "to learn that the permission our
committee gave Mr. Phillips to speak on Anti-Slavery last week has called out much unfavorable comment"—A storm of hisses and outcries from the abolitionists present interrupted and abashed the speaker.
"Do not misunderstand me," he cried, "it is not that
I personally objected to Mr. Phillips' remarks.
Quite the contrary, I assure you, quite the contrary!"
Hereupon the pro-slavery element began an uproar.
The poor man, unable to make himself heard, and
quite overcome by the demonstration, sat down help-
lessly and entirely forgot to introduce the speaker of

[56]

the evening. Mr. King, who had been an amused spectator of the scene, rose to his feet and advanced to the front of the stage. In stentorian tones that commanded attention he cried: "Ladies and gentlemen! My name is Thomas Starr King. I have come from Boston to read you a lecture to-night on 'The Laws of Disorder.' I am sure you will agree that this is a very opportune time for me to begin." The audience, captivated by the wit and tact of the speaker, laughed and applauded and settled down to listen.[1]

This incident brings to mind a characteristic trait of Mr. King, already referred to, his irrepressible humor and flow of spirits. He was "constitutionally hilarious," as some one has expressed it. He had the keenest eye for the odd, eccentric and ludicrous in the speech and conduct of his fellow-creatures. No one had such a fund of anecdotes and comical experiences, and no one could tell a story so inimitably. Once, when a matter-of-fact individual expostulated: "But, Mr. King, I was present on the occasion referred to, and saw no such happenings," the mirthful story-teller replied "Ah, but don't you

[1] A number of the most able and popular of Mr. King's lectures and pulpit discourses, after his death, by the advice of Frank Bret Harte, who had been charged with their examination, and in response to a general demand, were published in two volumes, entitled respectively "Substance and Show," and "Christianity and Humanity." They were edited, and prefaced by a felicitous, but all too brief memoir by his intimate friend Edwin P. Whipple. As Dr. Charles W. Eliot has said, they should be perused by every young American student of oratory, not only for their intellectual and moral values, but for their rhetorical quality, and the virility and beauty of their English style.

wish you could have?" Whenever any of this brilliant company of authors, lecturers and divines met each other, on the train speeding away to their respective appointments, or at the Old Corner Bookstore, or the dinners of the Examiner Club, there was a display of wit and wisdom that was worth listening to. In this blending of sense and nonsense, earnest and fun, Starr King was unequaled for spontaneity and brilliancy. This native mirthfulness appears especially in his voluminous correspondence, which overflows with quips, puns, good-natured banter, humorous sallies,—a well-spring of joy and cheer. Moreover, his wit, however telling, was so genial that it never wounded a heart or lost him a friend. I recall that at one of his Friday evening receptions in San Francisco the conversation turning to imperfections in speech, I shyly ventured to remark that I also had much difficulty with certain words— "There's 'Re-Religion.' Somehow, I stumble over it, I can't get it out!" With a look of pretended solicitude Mr. King rejoined, "How sad! Perhaps it's because you haven't it in you."

This keen sense of humor did a great deal to ease the friction and strain of life for Starr King, on whom this incessant round of clerical and literary engagements was beginning to tell most seriously. The profession of a lecturer, it has been truly said, is a most exhausting one. For five months in the year travelling over the country, enduring innumerable discomforts and exposures, sleeping in strange beds, eating

[58]

wife half frightened to pieces. She didn't get the despatch for which I paid a dollar.

"Last night I lectured in Concord. Emerson was there and heard 'Substance and Show.' I was terrified with his presence and didn't deliver it so well as usual. But he was stirred up, was quite eloquent in compliment and joy. He told the people my preaching wasn't so good as that. 'That *is* preaching,' he said to the Doctor of the village. I was really lifted up to find that he was so moved by the utterance. We had a supper at the Unitarian minister's after it was over. Emerson was there, and I entertained them with imitations of Beecher's preaching. I think Beecher's parish had better hire me for half the time to imitate Henry Ward's great sermons. Emerson was genial as a child and was in great humor over the imitations. Bellows at our church last Sunday, stirred our people up tremendously. He spoke without notes an hour and twenty minutes in the morning on Antioch College. Every man, woman and child was carried away as by a tempest. He could have raised $5000 if the contribution box had gone around after the sermon."

"February 9, 1855.

"I am home. Thank Heaven! I have escaped from the jaws of the West. I am *not* buried in snowdrifts, I am *not* frozen. I am *not* in my grave from dyspepsia. I am *not* starving on the train between Chicago and the Mississippi. I am *not* smashed up on the Ohio Central when two trains came nose to nose—but finding that I was on board concluded not to pitch into each other. I am not crazy from riding some ten nights without sleep. I am not quite desperate, although I lost $300 from my programme by storms and failures of engagements, and cleared only about $300. In a word I am not dead. Though why I am not, it would puzzle a metaphysician to determine. Such a journey! Catch me in the West again!

"To be sure I got glory, glory at Chicago, at Cincinnati, at Rockford; but I desire less glory and more comfort. I am home safe, after having almost seen the Mississippi, and quite plainly seen the Elephant. Instead of a trunk, however, he had a valise. When can I quit lecturing?"

One source of recuperation which delayed the impending break of his health was his summer vacation among the hills of New Hampshire and on the sea coasts of New England. He had an exquisite appreciation of natural scenery and an extraordinary talent for describing it. He knew the White Hills of New Hampshire better than their village guides and had explored the whole line of Cape Ann and the Massachusetts Coast. The fruit of his ten years' summering and wintering in our New England Alps was his letters to the *Boston Evening Transcript* on the New Hampshire Mountains, which, collected and revised, were later issued with illustrations in a volume, "The White Hills, their Legends, Landscape and Poetry,"—the single book he was spared to give to the public, a work of imaginative power and literary charm, and one which still holds its use as a guide-book and companion in that delightful region.

No man was so widely known as Mr. King in this mountain district and none more highly esteemed.

STARR KING MOUNTAIN, WHITE HILLS, NEW HAMPSHIRE
From Whitefield, N. H.

His graphic pen described its scenic beauty, his voice led public worship in its school houses and churches, his generous sympathy had been extended towards its poor. The noble peak, five thousand feet high, which overlooks the pleasant village of Jefferson, N. H., was named after him, Mt. Starr King. The precipitous and sombre King's ravine on the western slope of Mount Jefferson, which, in 1857, at the head of a party of mountaineers he was the first to explore, also perpetuates his memory to the dwellers and visitors in that region. At Gorham, where Mr. King passed nine summers, he was a familiar and beloved figure and remains an endeared tradition.

Many are the stories current in this mountain district of the wit and joyousness of these brilliant summer visitors. Once, when Dr. Chapin was engaged in playing a game of ten-pins, a bystander humorously remarked: "Why, Doctor Chapin, what would happen if your church people learned of your participation in this worldly amusement?" "Nothing whatever!" was the quick retort. "I should simply prove an alley-by."

Starr King, coming into the house one morning, reported: "It is raining like Caesar!" "An absurd comparison," said Chapin. "Not at all," rejoined King. "Have you so soon forgotten your classics— 'Caesar reigned hard.' "

When Henry Ward Beecher made one of the party, as not infrequently happened, the fun waxed fast and furious. Starr King used to tell of a long tramp the three friends once made through the mountains. Footsore and weary, at the close of a long hike, the daily stage-coach overtook them, and they quickly decided to avail themselves of it to reach their destination. Climbing to its top they distributed themselves, Starr King perching by the side of the driver and soon engaging him in a lively conversation. "Were you ever in New York?" he finally asked the unsuspecting Jehu. "Waal, I was onc't," the latter replied. "Some of my wife's folks invited us to visit 'em there two winters ago." "And did you enjoy it?" "I should say! Ain't it a big place? Nothin' to beat it this side o' kingdom come." "I suppose you were there over Sunday?" remarked Beecher. Yes, he had spent three Sundays in the great metropolis. "Where did you go to church on Sunday?" asked King. The stage driver lifted his eyebrows with surprise, and took another look at the dust-covered and slouchy trio ere he answered, "My wife's folks are Universalists, and the fust Sunday they took us to hear their crack preacher, Chapin." "And did you like him?" King asked mischievously. "Say now—he's a wonder. No use talking—he's a big man!" "Yes," retorted King, his eyes dancing with mirth, "you're right there. He's big enough. Almost as big as that man on the seat behind you." The driver craned his neck around for a fresh observation. "Bigger round the head; not so big in the stummic." There was a general explosion at this comment. Starr King persisted: "Didn't you go

[64]

to hear that other great preacher over in Brooklyn, Henry Ward Beecher?" "I did. Went to hear him to please my wife. She's a Congregational." "And did you like him?" "Sure! He's a stunner. Nothin' like him." "Well, now," asked King, "of those two men, Chapin and Beecher, which did you think was the greatest preacher?" "Sho," said the stage-driver, with an air of finality, "Beecher's a mighty smart man, but when it comes to preaching, Chapin can preach him right out of his boots!"

We permit ourselves to quote only two of the letters to personal friends in which Mr. King uttered the praises and sought to impart the charm of this lovely mountain region, to which he later did full justice in a widely read book.

To *Randolph Ryer:*

"May 30, 1853.

"I intimated to you last Monday morning that I might jump Anniversary Week by leaping over Boston into the district of the White Hills. Tuesday morning I made the attempt, arrived on Lake Winnipiseogee at noon, and after a most delicious sail dined at Centre Harbor. Started at 1:30 for Conway—roads good, no dust, mountains sharp in the sky as an axe, and air balmy and soft as the breezes of Paradise. Last fall I saw the hills in their October pomp; now the blossoms weighed the trees like vegetable snow, and the orchards seemed robed in bridal joy. After a most glorious and memorable ride we arrived in North Conway at evening, and slept at Thompson's under the protection of Mt. Kearsage. You remember our walk three years ago

[65]

in that village when the half-moon softened the landscape with its ethereal silver.

"Wednesday it stormed, but lifted at evening, giving us (I mean Rev. Chas. H. Leonard of Chelsea and myself) the privilege of a two hours' walk along the rich meadows that border the Saco. Thursday it stormed furiously and we were housed all day, with nothing to relieve the tedium. Friday morning was beautiful, inspiring, divine. We spent several hours exploring the beauties of North Conway, which is pronounced by artistic eyes, the loveliest village of New England. At 12 we started in an open wagon to go through the Pinkham road around the base of the Mt. Washington range to Gorham, N. H. The air was evidently the last remnant of the breeze that fanned Eden the morning after Eve was created; there never will be another like it till the new heavens and earth appear. O what a ride! Going through the village of Jackson, we saw the whole monarch range from base to summit at an angle that made us realize its height. Without going around the Eastern and Northern sides of the mountains it is impossible to know the majesty and magnificence of these hills. After riding some fifteen miles thus, we let the wagon return, and we walked seven miles carrying our overcoats and valises up hill much of the way. Pretty tough! Then we took a wagon and went to Gorham eight miles. The storm had torn the road very badly. It took us three hours to go the eight miles and we arrived at Gorham at 10:30 pretty well tired. Next morning we took a few hours to see the glorious aspects of the mountains from that side—very superior to anything on Gibbs' district, and at 11 started for home, which we reached at 8 P. M. Yesterday I preached on

[66]

'Blossoms,' suggested by the beauty of the trees amongst the mountains. Grand congregation. We think of boarding a few weeks at North Conway in a large farm house."

To the same:

"September 1, 1858.

"The summer is over. I send you an autumn greeting. This morning I arrived in Boston from Portland by boat. Yesterday forenoon I was driving in a wagon far up on the banks of the Androscoggin within twenty miles of Umbagog lake, and feasting my eyes on the noble view of the three greatest mountains of the White Mountain range—Washington, Jefferson, and Madison. It is a view which I discovered this year, and it beats all other landscape views of the hills out and out. No visitors of the region have ever seen it except such as I have taken there. Up to this year the Creator of all Mountains has enjoyed it almost exclusively.

"I have been at the mountains nearly eight weeks. Was worn out when I came. Am now hearty, and shouldn't know that I had written or spoken for a year.

"I have been to Franconia twice, to the Notch district twice, to Dixville Notch once, to North Conway once, to Lancaster and the Connecticut river once, and to Berlin Falls twenty times. Also once to the Snow Arch in Tuckerman's ravine, twice to the summit of Mt. Washington (staying all night once), and twice to the top of Mt. Hayes—also to the top of Mt. Lafayette in Franconia. So I have had a somewhat ample feast of mountain splendor."

Aside from this communion with nature his chief

[67]

diversion was the love of the arts; especially of music, of which he had the most exquisite appreciation, as his letters and his noble lecture on Music bear witness.[1] An even more striking testimony to his artistic sensibility is afforded by the action of a group of some forty leading artists of Boston—many distinguished painters and sculptors among them—who on receiving the sad intelligence of Starr King's death, printed in the *Boston Evening Transcript* an appreciative tribute to him as one who by his eloquent word-pictures of Nature's beauty and sublimity, and his enlightened understanding of Art as its interpreter to the human soul, had placed them under great and unforgettable obligations.

[1] In "Substance and Show," p. 231.

CHAPTER IV

CALL AND TRANSFER TO CALIFORNIA

IT became apparent that after eleven years of this exhaustive service Starr King needed a change of environment, a new field of labor where he would be able to make larger use of his literary capital, and gain the income needed to support his family and meet his naturally expensive tastes and large charities. Various cities sought him as pastor, Brooklyn, Cincinnati and Chicago among them. He felt himself most attracted by a call from the young and struggling Unitarian Church in San Francisco. The romantic history and imposing scenery of California, the pledge of an adequate salary which would preclude the necessity of a recourse to the "detestable vagrancy of lecturing," as he called it; above all, the challenge to his missionary zeal and consecration powerfully appealed to him. This deeper ethical and religious motive prevailed. "I do think," he wrote his friend Dr. Henry W. Bellows of New York, "we are unfaithful in huddling so closely around the cosy stove of civilization in this blessed Boston, and I, for one, am ready to go out into the cold and see if I am good for anything."

The first intimation of this decision given to his

[69]

friends we find in a letter written to Randolph Ryer under date of September, 1859.

"I have lots of things to tell you, among others that I shall probably move to San Francisco. The White Mountain book will be out for the holidays. It will be a beauty. As to California, read the enclosed letter. I have thought best to let you see just what I wrote the committee.

"'I shall go to you in the hope of using all the powers that may be continued to me for your permanent strength as a Liberal Christian parish. My great ambition in life is to serve the cause of Christianity as represented by the noblest souls of all the Liberal Christian parties. I am not conscious of any gifts, either of thought or speech, that can make my presence with you so desirable as you seem to think; but if I can be of service by cooperating with you in laying deeper the foundations and lifting higher the walls of our faith in your city, whose civilization is weaving out of the most various and in many respects the best threads of the American character, I shall have reason always to bless Providence for a rich privilege.'"

Mr. King's decision to remove to San Francisco awoke a storm of regrets and remonstrances from his parishioners and friends. His Boston congregation could not bring themselves to consent to a permanent separation, and finally a vacation was extended to him for fifteen months, during which time the society would depend on pulpit supplies from Sunday to Sunday, in the hope that their beloved minister would

[70]

return to them at the expiration of his leave of absence. On Sunday, the 25th of March, 1860, before a crowded audience, Mr. King preached his farewell sermon, "Words at Parting," a moving utterance of affection and gratitude.

At a social gathering of the parish he received so many manifestations of the love with which they cherished him that his resolution to leave them almost gave way. A further trial of his loyalty awaited him in New York, where, the day before the sailing of the steamer that was to bear him and his family on their journey to the far Pacific Coast, a public dinner and reception was given in his honor at the Fifth Avenue Hotel by the Unitarian laity and clergy of that city. Three hundred guests were seated at the tables. The venerable poet William Cullen Bryant presided. Revs. Bellows, Osgood, Farley, Samuel Longfellow, O. B. Frothingham, and others, made addresses. The report of the speeches and proceedings, including Starr King's response, filled fourteen columns of the *New York Christian Inquirer*. As E. P. Whipple says, two short sentences in the letter sent the committee by Rev. Dr. F. H. Hedge, one of the most intimate of his friends, condensed the spirit which animated the assembly: "King is with you for a parting word, and your fraternal benediction on his way. Happy soul! himself a benediction wherever he goes, benignly dispensing the graces of his life wherever he carries the wisdom of his word."

[71]

On the fifth of April, 1860, Thomas Starr King, with his wife and little daughter Edith, sailed on the steamship *Northern Light,* by way of the Isthmus of Panama, for his new and chosen field of labor.

Mr. King kept a detailed journal of the voyage for the information of his own and his wife's relatives, and Boston friends. Sundry extracts from it will be of interest. The present writer made the same journey in the following year under similar conditions, and can vouch for the accuracy of Mr. King's descriptions of the scenery and other features of the transit across the Isthmus, and the discomforts and miseries to which the traveller was subjected in those early days by the barriers created by an unsubdued nature, and the rapacity of ship-owners and their agents.

"NEW YORK HARBOR, April 5th, 1860.

"The *Northern Light* was to sail at 12 precisely. . . . We did not reach the ship as early as we intended. Horace Greeley came to see me at the Fifth Avenue Hotel in the morning to give me the names of the people I must know in California and some practical advice. 'You are going,' he said, 'to a divine country. There is nothing like it on the face of the earth. You will be fascinated by it, except San Francisco, which I think,' said he, 'has the worst climate, and is the most infernal hole on the face of the earth.' A pretty attractive character to give my future home! There were lots of little last things to be done. We did not leave the hotel until nearly ten. Rev. E. H. Chapin rode down in the carriage with us, and left us at the pier in order to attend a funeral. Several ministers were in waiting to say farewell. Mr. Samuel Longfellow and Dr. Farley of Brooklyn, Mr. A. A. Livermore of the *Inquirer,* Octavius B. Frothingham, and Mr. Barrett, the Swedenborgian. Lots of other friends were in attendance. My constant friend Randolph Ryer was, of course, on hand. What shall I do without him in San Francisco? Wm. C. Martin, a large lump of the very finest salt on the earth, was there. Then there were the Boston brethren. It is a luxury to write their names—Edward H. Eldredge, Warren Sawyer, Joseph Greeley, John Stetson and Baker Welch. How absurd it seems to leave such attachment as these men have shown me! Friendship enough to bless a dozen men better than I am a whole life-time has been poured out from them towards me the last three months. I am glad no more of the parish were present to make the parting sharper. Our dear friend Thomas B. Fox was also in the state-room when we reached the steamer, to bid us farewell. To be sure, he might have been seen at the same moment in his little fountain office on Washington Street, where the *Christian Examiner's* eloquence bubbles up into the literature of the world. But the real, genuine, substantial Fox was with us in spirit, and sent a splendid bouquet of flowers to keep his memory fragrant on the first days of the voyage."

"AT SEA, April 7th.

"We are beyond Hatteras and across the Gulf Stream. The passengers, a vast number of whom were sick yesterday, are all out this morning. And what a crowd! There are a thousand persons on this moderate sized steamship. It is almost impossi-

[73]

ble to walk the narrow passageways in front of our state-room doors, the only open air promenade the ship affords. We are packed in like cattle in a stock train. Just twice as many as the boat can accommodate are jammed into her. It is infamous and it is frightful. There are only four small boats attached to the ship, not enough to save the children in case of accident. I do not see any life preservers anywhere. Old Vanderbilt ought to be dragged after the ship in the sea, like a ship-mop, from New York to Aspinwall. The stories of wrong, extortion and outrage as to tickets told by the persons on board show that he is a shark packed into human shape and baptized with a Christian name."

"AT SEA, April 8th.

"A glorious Sunday morning, the sky unclouded, the sea a brilliant azure, and flecked with white caps which tell us we have still a pleasant breeze. We are off Florida, yet the air is not the least oppressive. The passengers want me to preach. There is no other minister on board. Heaven knows there are people enough for three congregations. I preached on Proverbs iv, 23, taking the capstan for a pulpit. It was a severe strain upon the voice to speak in the open air against the noise of the steamer. There was a large gathering and a very attentive one.

"The Southern Cross is certainly a poetic and inspiring spectacle, but by association rather than in reality. It needs one more star in it on the long beam of the cross. If I could improve the firmament, I would nail one there. It is larger than I imagined, but anybody who sails beyond the Great Bear to see it makes a bad investment. Last night we had both in the sky. It is amusing to note the *ennui* of people who can't read, write or think. One passenger to-day sat with a very down-cast countenance, then yawned and said: "Oh, God! If I could only go to work once more and work all day like the Devil!"

"AT ASPINWALL, April 13th, 1860.

"We reached the harbor of Aspinwall on the Isthmus before daylight this morning, having made the passage from New York in 7 days, 18 hours. There is very little twilight in the low latitudes, and it was not until sunrise, that we saw the vegetation which clothed the flat curving coast around the steamer. The first burst of sunshine kindled up a vast extent of verdure of a more vivid poll-parrot-y tone in its green that I have ever seen before. The first object that fastened my eyes was a grove of cocoanut trees; their branches spread out from the top of their trunks. They look precisely like huge peacock feathers, and when the breeze pitched them about, they looked like the hair of an uncombed boy, blown by the wind *every which way.'* Two U. S. steamers were lying at anchor in the harbor of Aspinwall. A boat load of their sailors, in full blue, rowed past our ship to the wharf. Edith, who was on the watch for all novelties, exclaimed, 'Father, there are the natives, what queer looking people!' In ten minutes after we reached the wharf, 900 people had jumped ashore from our vessel, and rushed to the various little hotels and eating rooms. The cars were to leave about 7.30 a. m. for Panama. We stayed on board to pack up our score or two of bundles, just gaining the train in season, and at 7.30 started for the Pacific. The steerage passengers had been sent in a train ahead. There were 8 cars filled with the first and second cabin travellers, each car

[75]

seating more than 60. The Railroad Company received $25 for each passenger and 10 cents per lb. for all luggage over 50 lbs. for each person. The two trains this morning paid them over $25,000. The distance across the Isthmus from ocean to ocean is about 48 miles. We were about 3 hours by the cars on the passage. I did not sit down the whole way, but stood in the doorway, and on the platform to enjoy all that possibly could be seen of the new landscape. It was very striking certainly; and yet I must confess to a little disappointment. It was not the Isthmus of my imagination, chiefly because the colors were not as rich as I had anticipated. But the rainy season has not yet set in. The flowers, I presume, do not enliven the forest with their bloom until the rains of May and June water the soil. Still the ride was crammed with interest. We plunged into a tropic swamp at once on leaving Aspinwall, and rushed through the characteristic leafage of the lands near the Equator. Orange and lemon trees, palms with great bunches of red nuts from which the palm oil is extracted, drooping from them; cocoanut trees; cottonwoods; mahogany trees; India-rubber trees, with vines running off from their high tops to the ground, like the cordage from a tall mast; all sorts of queer rank ferns and shrubbery, with the huge banana leaf generally overtopping them as if in glee that nothing else could grow so fast; and here and there a large tree like a leviathan lilac with no leaves, but bursting from every twig-point with yellow and crimson splendor. Such was the kind of feast through which we were whirled. The day was not so oppressive in heat, as I feared it might be. There was breeze enough to save us from suffocation. I have often suffered twice as much from heat in a ride from Boston to Portland in June. The most fascinating portions of the ride were the negro huts and their surroundings. Here and there, we came upon a white, pine, Yankee house, with bright green blinds, and perhaps a bar with bad liquor to sell. Some employè of the road, probably, was tenant. It was a sad blotch upon the tropic wilderness, with its uncouth shape, and its dazzling blaze in the powerful sunshine. But the negro huts were charming. They were mostly sheds, roofed very tastily with dry palm leaves. They looked quite cool among the bananas, cocoanuts and thriving palms of the garden spot that generally surrounds them; now and then they were embowered in splendid flowering vines. The negro children in the doorways were usually naked. Almost all of them were as corpulent as little aldermen, showing that they take life easy, and laugh and grow fat. A large portion of the men were three-quarters naked. Their skins were certainly the finest in hue and seemingly in texture, I have ever seen. They looked like images cast in golden bronze. Whether they are Nubians or a cross between the native Indian and the negro, I could not learn, but they certainly are the most splendid specimens of color in human shape I have fallen in with, and put the Caucasian hue to shame. That is the color Providence intends for the tropics. It harmonizes with the scenery. The Venus and Apollo of that latitude, should not be marble figures, but vital, moving figures. We followed the windings of the Chagres River for 30 miles. The immigrants, 10 or 12 years ago, were taken up this stream in boats, hundreds of them catching fever on the passage. The scenery must have been extremely fascinating then,—when the swamps had not been invaded by axe or fire, and the windings of the stream were opening continual surprises of the richest foliage and bloom. As we approached the Pacific coast, we could see mountain heights, green to the summit, through openings in the forest. The foliage was less interesting the last quarter of the way; yet the excitement increased, for we were soon to see the blue bosom of the *other ocean*.

"AT PANAMA.

"As soon as the mile posts indicated 'five miles' to the terminus, I kept a sharp look-out, leaning over the step of the car on the platform. At last a sharp turn showed a huge cocoanut tree, whose flaunting top was flashing in the light, and directly beyond it the two towers of an old time-stained cathedral. Beyond was an expanse of azure sleeping in the hot noon. This was Panama, slowly crumbling into picturesqueness on the shore of its lovely Pacific bay. The view gave us a moment of poetry, but it was followed by an hour of decided prose. Such a rush and crush as there was, when our 500 souls poured from the train. Almost everybody had some package or heap of traps to be carried by hand. And we were all to be packed on a little ferry boat, which would take us out over the shoal bay, three miles to the steamer in waiting. I hired two negroes, loaded them with camp stools, shawls, overcoats, bottles of cider, pots of pickled oysters, a package of crackers, and a large French valise, and we struck for the boat. When we had been pushed by the crowd half way up to the boat, I discovered that our carpet bag with lots of clean clothing, my dressing case and some sermons in it had been left behind. I dispatched Sarah Kennedy to find it, and we were borne

[78]

on by the living tide to the ferry boat. The gangway was about two feet wide, and through this, which kept swaying by the tide, we were to be squeezed into the boat. This was the most trying operation of the voyage. At last the feat was accomplished, and we found ourselves wedged into the mass of beings on the deck. Soon Sarah returned with the bag, and we were off for the steamer. We had in tow a huge scow on which the steerage passengers were freighted like a swarm of bees; and thus we went, a thousand human beings, women looking disconsolate, men swearing, lots of people frightened from fear we should upset, everybody separated from the person he or she wanted, nobody able to move, children crying, babies screaming—to the boat that was to take us to San Francisco. In half an hour we were alongside. We were told in the New York office, that we should connect with the *Golden Age* or the *John L. Stephens.* Either of them would have been large enough to accommodate our cabin passengers. It was the *Sonora,* the smallest, oldest, slowest, dirtiest boat of the four chief ones on this side. The *Sonora* had not state-rooms enough. Fifty first-class passengers must be without rooms. We found, too, on arrival, that we were not to leave at once. We must wait for the arrival of the New Orleans boat at Aspinwall, and the transfer of her passengers and mails to our boat. This will certainly detain us a day, perhaps longer,—an arrangement which is one of the beauties of the new combination with Vanderbilt.

"Last evening was delightful as we lay still in the Bay of Panama. It is a most lovely sheet of water. The town, with its old cathedral towers, is about 2 miles from the ship's anchorage. There are several rocky walled islands near, and back from the city rise charming mountain heights and ranges, some very high ones stretching back in the hot haze, while in front of the curving harbor, sleeps the blue Pacific. The water setting resembles the shores of Lake Winnipiseogee more than any other spot I have ever seen. One distant mountain was almost a duplicate in shape of Chocorua. Another height strangely resembled the swell and summits of the Belknap Hills, and the irregular forms strongly remind one of the mountain rim that holds that gem of New Hampshire. But there is a richer color steadily swathing these island mountains. The foliage on them in the distance has a crisp and knotted look, making you think of hair done up in curl papers. There is more fire in the color. The hills of New Hampshire are more like cool emeralds, or pale sapphires, in their natural quality. These are big rubies, and seem ready at the right angle of light, to glow ruddy through and through. After the calm sunset we watched for the phosphorescence on the water. The waters of the harbor are famous for it and we were not disappointed. Other waters sparkle with this phosphorus, but these seem to be a mass of gleaming silver,—a lake of quicksilver. A boat was tethered to our steamer by a small rope which lay a foot deep in the water. As it swayed up and down it seemed to be a silver cord rising and falling on the gentle swell. Every dip of an oar, when a boat went by us, turned up liquid light. Splash the water and it made a spatter of stars. Dip your hand in it and as the stream ran off, your fingers were lambent with the strange flame. There were lots of pelicans flying about the bay. They would rise several rods above the water, and suddenly drop down, as if they were shot, splashing up the water beautifully, and sinking in it after some fish, which was quickly transferred from the large pouch of the Pacific to the smaller pouch of the pelican. I watched them a long while on the hot morning, and came to the conclusion that it is hard work to get a living on this globe. A pelican certainly works his passage, but I suppose it is 'attractive industry.' I was really sorry to leave Panama. But we have kept the shore in sight all the afternoon. Our course is still South, in order to clear the headlands of the bay, which stretch southwest. We shall be within 400 miles of the base of Chimborazo, before morning. How I wish the steamer would run down there before heading for San Francisco."

"ON THE PACIFIC, Sunday, April 15th.

"The passengers insisted upon having service. I preached a Palm Sunday service on 'Jesus a King' from Luke 19th, 25th, etc. The preaching was in the dining saloon, and persons on the guards outside could hear through the windows. There was a large attendance, fine singing,—and preaching nothing more than poor. There was a whale in sight to-day. He spurted and leaped, showing his flippers quite near the steamer. This evening the sunset was superb, the colors, particularly the green, deep between the cirrus clouds, were of marvellous beauty. Julia has not been sick to-day, but she does not go to the table, eats very little and very daintily, and seems to be afflicted with a strange, nervous wretchedness on deck. She was not made for a sailor, and does not enjoy a single sight or moment on the ocean. Edith is as frisky as a colt, and as much at home on the steamer as if she were in Burroughs Place or with

[81]

Grandmother Wiggin. I forgot to state that I was put as room-mate with Mr. Lambert and Mr. Brooks, two of the trustees of the Unitarian Society in San Francisco."

"AT SEA, Sunday, April 22.

"I preached at 10:30 this morning in the dining saloon. It is a hard trial to the voice to speak in the low, long room, and against the dull, plodding sound of the machinery and wheels. A large number attended. The text was Psalm xlii: 1, a favorite text with me.—'As the hart panteth after the water-brooks, so panteth my heart after thee, O God.' But it seemed to me as though all the vitality of the sermon, and of all possible preaching is taken out by the restricted limits, and the dull roar in the ears. I wonder if any soul was ever saved, where the man was obliged to hold his hand to his ear and lost an important word now and then. In the afternoon I preached in the steerage. Service was at 2 o'clock. I spoke without notes, preaching from John xvi, 33.—'In the world ye shall have tribulation; but be of good cheer, I have overcome the world.' I stood on the upper deck near the bow, with my back to it, and the breeze carried the voice forward very kindly. There was a large attendance, and the assembly seemed very attentive and reverent. There were two or three Methodist local preachers or exhorters among the steerage passengers and they led the singing, which was strong and hearty. There was no awning. I spoke with my hat off under the high sun and with my hair blowing like the cocoanut leaves. I spoke more easily and with better command of the subject than I expected; but so feebly in comparison with the power of a genuine born extem-

[82]

pore speaker. How Beecher would have done it! I was not made for such address; but I enjoyed the service far more than in the cabin, and am very glad I was called to it. I found several intelligent men among the hearers, and had a long talk with them afterwards. They say that there are at least 500 in the steerage. (The officers confess to only 300.) And they say, too, that many of the passengers paid $150, $160, and $170 for their tickets, in the regular office too in New York. This evening the sky was glorious. It was the richest night yet. The new moon, visible on the very horizon, and with horns up, sank like a silver gondola, towards the Sandwich Islands. Venus was as large as a peach and washed acres of the sea with gentle splendor. Jupiter glowed like a white coal nearly in the zenith. On one side of the ship was the north star, low in the sky, overhung by the brilliant dipper upside down. On the other side the Southern Cross. The whole southern portion of the heavens was strewn with magnificent stars. It was the most lustrous night I have ever seen. 'He telleth the number of the stars: He calleth them all by their names.'"

There follows in his journal a vivid description of the visit and sojourn of the vessel in the harbor of Acapulco, Mexico; but it is too long for insertion here. Mr. King continued his record of daily experiences until the arrival of the steamship at its destination.

"IN PORT, Monday, April 30th.

"We are in San Francisco! The passage into the bay through the Golden Gate was very interesting. The passage is made between rocks on one side and

a steep mountain on the other. The mountain has no trees, but was covered to the top with a carpet of flowers, wild flowers. There were more flowers than green. The hues were violet, yellow, red, and saffron, and the effect was inexpressibly charming. It was as striking as our October tints, but as different as possible, being literally a carpet, or rather a huge plushy, richly wrought rug. There was not a stone on the mountain side to mar the soft and pleasant effect. Julia did not lift her head from the berth, to see anything as we went in. She was not moved to be dressed until the steamer was moored. Then she was lifted and carried out. The committee of the parish were in waiting on the pier and gave me as hearty a reception as could be imagined. They had given notice there would be no service on the Sunday, under the impression that I should be too tired or weak to preach. But I induced them to countermand the order, although it was 3 o'clock P. M. when we reached the pier. Julia was taken in charge at once in a carriage, and we drove to the Oriental Hotel, a forlorn looking wooden building in a wretched part of the city, but the best kept house in the place. We have a sitting room with two bad-smelling bed-rooms leading from it. A few minutes after we sat down, we had a box of magnificent strawberries sent to us, or rather to Julia, and a splendid bouquet, with compliments of Mrs. Otis. The berries were very large and were delicious. Yesterday morning was superb. There were no clouds, and it was not hot. Although notice was given only in a Sunday morning paper of the service, the church was crowded; every aisle was full, and a hundred went away unable to get in. The singing was excellent. The sermon seemed to impress the people, and the parish appear to be in the highest spirits. They take up a contribution here at each service in addition to the pew rents. The collection yesterday was $100. There was no service in the evening. This morning I drove out before breakfast to see the country within a few miles. The flowers in the fields are wonderful in their mass, color and variety. That is all that has impressed me favorably as yet. The city is very queer, and very uninteresting to Eastern eyes. It is a vast struggle of houses over half a dozen sand hills, and the streets are bilious with Chinamen. But I can't tell as yet how, or what, I shall like. Julia is better, and is fast regaining strength by firm land, rest and eating. The living at the hotel is very good. The 'overland mail' closes in half an hour, and I must stop suddenly to get these hasty sheets off. We have every call to be grateful for preservation on the sea from storm and fire, and for the friends that welcome us in this far off post by the Pacific.

"*Te Deum Laudamus.*"

CHAPTER V

THE NEW FIELD IN SAN FRANCISCO

THOMAS STARR KING, as we have seen, entered the Golden Gate on Saturday, the 28th of April, 1860, and the next morning the Unitarian Church, on Stockton near California Street, was filled with a large and eager audience of intelligent and influential citizens of San Francisco, to whom he preached a sea-written discourse on the text: "And they shall come from the east and the west, and from the north and from the south, and shall sit down in the Kingdom of God." Mr. King in a letter to a friend [1] thus describes his first impressions. "I felt lonely enough and yet hopeful. I couldn't help crying like a baby when I first went into the pulpit in thinking of all that I had left behind at the east, and then, I hope, I cried no less intensely to the Lord. The weather on Sunday was Italian; since then it has been the wretchedest possible, after the Boston type. I have not, therefore, seen anything yet but the dreary, decrepit-looking city. But I shall like it here, I am sure. Preaching I shall enjoy as never before. The parish are in high spirits. The mammon side of the establishment

[1] Rev. A. A. Livermore.

[86]

is already successful. It remains to be seen if we can serve the other master."

In the congregation assembled to listen to him that morning the expectation was great. When he edged his way down the closely packed aisles to the pulpit the disappointment of his hearers was general. "Could this slender, youthful looking man, with his beardless, boyish face and long, lank hair, be the celebrated preacher, Thomas Starr King?" And, indeed, Mr. King's personal appearance was not calculated to impress you with his talent and power. He used to complain humorously that his want of size especially told against him in that country of big waterfalls, big trees and big vegetables. "But," he would add humorously, "though I weigh only 120 pounds, when I am mad I weigh a ton!"

The Hindu Theist, J. C. Gangooly, one of the first of the Brahmin fraternity to visit America, was once invited by Mr. King to address his congregation at Hollis Street. Looking around him admiringly Gangooly began: "You have a beautiful church. You have a most excellent minister. And what a noble name he bears! Starr, a luminary in the heavens; King, a ruler among men!" Then turning around in the pulpit to Mr. King sitting behind him, he added, "Well, he does not look it!"

As that morning he put on the ministerial gown which he always wore in the pulpit, partly, perhaps, to round out his deficient physical proportions, all eyes were fixed upon him with suspense. But the

[87]

moment the tones of his rich and resonant voice were heard the anxiety was dispelled, and confidence and delight took its place, which the exercises and sermon confirmed. From that first Sunday Starr King's reputation as an orator was established in San Francisco. Crowds attended the Sunday services and his fame spread all over the state. Not a few came quite regularly every Saturday night by river boat from Sacramento and other interior points to hear his Sunday discourses. His parish was soon unequaled in the city for the social and business standing, and the intellectual and moral worth of its membership.

Not long after his arrival Mr. King set about clearing off the accumulated indebtedness of the church, which amounted to some $20,000. Having succeeded in this he began a subscription towards a new and larger church edifice, which was urgently needed, raising in all some $80,000 towards this object. In return Mr. King's San Francisco parishioners sent him on Christmas Day, 1860, a splendid service of silver, as an expression of their good will and gratitude.

Mr. King's own impressions of his new field of labor are recorded in letters to his eastern friends.

"By Pony Express,
"SAN FRANCISCO, May 11th, 1860.
"My dear Fox: [1]
"I send you a word of greeting through the Rocky

[1] Rev. Thomas B. Fox, one of the editors of the *Boston Evening Transcript.*

Mountains. Is not the Pony Express a right-down California institution? Snorting through the passes of the Rocky Mountains at a rate that beats the steamers 8 days in getting letters through to New York and Boston. Prices are moderate, $5 a letter, cheap for the luxury of writing to you. I would pay $10 to see you. My wife would contribute another, no doubt. But it would require more than two 'eagles'' wings to bring you here by sea, or over the great crests where the eagles roost.

"You have seen my journal, which probably told you how we fared and when we arrived. We have been here two weeks to-morrow. The parish enterprise is already successful beyond the most sanguine expectations of the leaders. The income of the society will pay my salary and leave a large surplus to sponge off something of the debt. It is a noble place to preach in, and they need it. The city as a place to live in—*O mein Gott!* As a business centre and illustration of the magic of Yankee enterprise, Aladdin's lamp feats are pale before it. And it is something like the Aladdin business. For this city has been four times burned down. But the harder the rubs, the more miraculous the magic here. I have been some fifty miles into the country already and have seen some scenery that could not be surpassed for color. I shall enjoy my work here, and the country will be a perpetual resource and delight.

" I forgot to thank you elaborately for your admirable White Mountain article, and your friendly but excessive praise of the author's work. The book won't pay me pecuniarily (I have not realized $500 from it, and its sale, I suspect, is about over) but it has paid me in compliments and kind words, among which yours are chief and welcome. You spoke of a

[89]

letter of mine in the *Transcript* on the Bay as good. Singularly I received at the same time a letter from a friend of taste, in Boston, who thought I must be seriously sick, as that letter was so poor. . . . But how charming K. C.'s pieces are! I read them with constant delight and admiration. They ought to be printed one of these days. Then my book will be in shadow.

"I dined the other day with the new Republican Senator from Oregon, Col. Baker, at Col. Fremont's. Baker and I arranged for a hunting party in Oregon among the great Cascade Mountains, next June. I am a missionary and shall carry the Gospel to the deer people. Mrs. Jessie Fremont was here last evening to show us the medal and decorations sent to her husband from Berlin this week, with news of his election into an order there. He takes the place of Macaulay. Yours in exile,

"T. S. K."

To *Randolph Ryer:*

"SAN FRANCISCO, August 5th, 1860.

"If I am to be absent two years, one-sixth of the time has passed. I can't say that I look forward with jubilance to a stay here five times as long in the future. But I feel very sure that I shall not get away in less time than that. I want to see all the debt of the society paid, a new organ bought, a new church-front erected, a new parish started in another part of the city, and a good man invited and on hand to step into my place. Will not this require full two years? I think so. Last Wednesday I spoke to the negroes on Emancipation Day, and had a rich time. You would have been fully satisfied with the eloquence of the sable admirer who introduced me. He described

[90]

me as riding on the livid lightnings of my eloquence over the Sierras, and carried out beyond the coruscations of the galaxies, and hoped that in my dying *apathy,* when I caught a glimpse of my *terrestial* home, I might soar on the wings of immortal mind to the Infinite that would be anxiously awaiting me.   It was great!   Thank you for the sermons on Theodore Parker by James Freeman Clarke and O. B. Frothingham.   The last is the most able analysis of Parker's gifts that I have seen.   I, also, spoke of Parker in a sermon which I once decided to print, but reconsidered."

To his friend Alger he wrote some months later:

"SAN FRANCISCO, November 5th, 1860.

"Yesterday was Sunday; and yet the *Sonora* dared to steam into port, having no fear of Presbyterian indignation, and brought the mail, of which your letter was the gem.   After preaching to a full congregation in the morning, I refreshed myself thoroughly with your wise and friendly words, that lost no particle of worth or flavor in their flight of six thousand miles.   I am deeply indebted for the privilege of a peep through your stereoscope at Martineau embracing Dr. Dewey.   How exquisite, yet sad, the music of their duet!   The only quarrel I have with the government of this Universe is that such men can't have the power—or their friends for them—of buying up the vitality of a score or so of worthless creatures, that they may be kept in the maturity of their glorious genius here for two or three generations.   Some Ponce de Leon will yet discover the pool in which the intellectual aristocracy can thus be rejuvenated.   But think of Dr. N. A. taking a bath in it, and holding over for a century to lecture to us on Gehenna!

"The weather here is delightful now. We have had some showers in October, and the hills are showing a tint of green. It is our spring time. Every day we are out without overcoats; the scenery surrounding the city is inspiring with beauty. Mt. Diablo is visible from the gate at my front yard, and strongly resembles Mt. Washington seen from Winnipiseogee. It is a superb dessert to my breakfast every morning — bearing up a dome nobly moulded and graciously adorned with flashing grey, and violet shadows, back of a long, torn range of hills into the sky. From my library windows we see the range of hills that heave up from the Pacific, and east of them 40 miles of the dreaming bay. I miss Boston more and more, and yet my feeling is not homesickness. Am I beginning to feel the fascination of this region, which they say, unfits one for living anywhere else, although we may feel eager now and then to get away?

"Our church continues full. In the evening our own people generally stay at home, and yet the seats are all filled with strangers. So I preach to a double-barrelled congregation. Monday evenings I have a large class for religious instruction. We meet in the church. About 200 attend regularly. I lecture extempore for an hour on Matthew."

The writer has sometimes pondered what it was that so attracted the average man and woman of that day to Mr. King's preaching. He had certainly in no sense a popular style in the pulpit. His discourses, all read from the manuscript, were mostly on phil-

[92]

osophical and spiritual themes, and were classical
in form, elegant, even ornate, in language, and digni-
fied and chaste in delivery. There were no let-
downs in them, or other concessions to the vulgar
taste. This elevation and spirituality naturally edi-
fied the more intelligent and religiously inclined
among his hearers. In those days the sermon was
still regarded as literature. The preacher considered
it as not simply a work of edification, but of art, ap-
pealing not only to man's intellect, conscience and
heart, but to his sense of the beautiful also. The
congregations Starr King addressed were for the
most part thoughtful, well educated and serious.
Religion was to them not a fleeting sentiment, a
momentary impression, but the transfiguration
of the entire life by ethical ideals and spiritual
trusts.

The solemnity and beauty of his prayers, the remarkable impressiveness of his reading of Scripture
and hymn, and the electric quality of his delivery
were to others the great attraction. He possessed a
marvellous voice, deep and rich, with great carrying
power. No one that ever heard it but recalls its fascination. His dark, luminous eyes, too, were wonderfully expressive; "living sermons," some one
called them. It is in the delivery that the success of
the orator consists, as Goethe reminds us. In the case
of Starr King nature had to a rare degree endowed
him for his rhetorical task.

These rhetorical powers were strikingly displayed

[93]

also in a private club formed for the reading and study of Shakespeare. The plays were read, book in hand, with the proper dramatic entrances and exits. Mr. King, Col. Lippitt, Mrs. Hastings— a sister of United States Senator Charles Sumner and a superb reader, and Horace Davis, son of Governor John Davis of Massachusetts, a man of varied culture and eminent public service, who later married Mr. King's daughter Edith, were among the more prominent members of this gifted circle. The writer will never forget the impressive recitals of Macbeth, Coriolanus, King Lear, and other plays, rendered by this talented company which he was permitted to attend.

Mr. King at once identified himself with the higher interests of California society. From the moment he stepped upon its soil, he felt himself to be a citizen of the Golden State. Looking beyond the pulpit he mingled much with men, touching life at all points. In society he displayed a rare tact and charm, meeting his fellow beings of whatever condition on the plane of their everyday feelings and pursuits. His ready sympathies were enlisted in behalf of all who were in distress or need, and his doors constantly beset with applicants for his counsel and bounty, to whom he gave himself but too generously. For years he kept an account of his expenditures, setting down on one page his outlays for pleasure, recreation, and self-indulgence of every sort, and on the opposite his gifts for good causes and charity.

[94]

The balance, we may be sure, was always kept on the side of altruism and humanity.

The struggling philanthropies of San Francisco, of all creeds and kinds, soon discovered his disinterestedness and readiness to become an eloquent beggar in their behalf. To all alike he gave his services cheerfully and lavishly, for he was as opulent in benefactions as the sun. The Seamen's Bethel, orphan asylums, temperance societies, Masonic Relief Boards, child-saving institutions, mission Sunday Schools, and especially the churches of the colored people, found their causes effectively presented and their treasuries enriched by his appeals. His broad and catholic spirit especially fitted him for such a service, for while he knew the necessity for, and the value of denominations, he looked beyond them to the great universal principles of religion and ethics, and dwelt with preference on the central unities rather than the incidental diversities of Christian faith. Almost the sole representative of Liberal Christianity in that new community, he felt it incumbent upon him to do all in his power to advance its principles and interests. Before crowded audiences in his church he gave a series of twelve lectures, each an hour or more in length, on the distinctive doctrines of the liberal faith which necessitated and justified its separate existence. But he was always glad to recognize the good in other creeds and churches, and ever sought to build his denominational fences so low that he and they could freely shake

[95]

hands across them. A few weeks before his death he had arranged for the occupancy of his pulpit on a Sunday by Dr. Cohn, a distinguished Hebrew Rabbi.

That his more orthodox neighbors did not always reciprocate this broad churchmanship, but sometimes displayed toward him a narrow and bigoted temper never disturbed the charity of his judgments or the generosity of his deeds towards them.

More trying to his sensitive nature were the unjust criticisms made upon him by certain members of his own congregation who, instead of rejoicing in his larger activities in the community, deprecated the attention he gave to public and patriotic causes, and desired him to confine himself more to their personal and parish interests. On one occasion, at least, Mr. King opened his heart to me on this subject, and spoke with profound sorrow of the unreasonableness and unkindness of these advocates of a parochial and sectarian policy on the part of their minister.

Writing to Edward Everett Hale he confesses: "The public spirit here is poor, and the church spirit narrower than in any community I ever dealt with. I have no influence within the citadel, but I am bishop of the unfortunate expanse without. Methodism Unitarianized, or Unitarianism Methodized, is just the combination for this longitude. There is the right mingling of fire and cylinder, steel and steam."

On the 31st of January, 1861, the Hollis Street

Church in Boston observed the fiftieth anniversary of the dedication of its "meeting house" by a public gathering at which addresses were made by Revs. Dr. F. H. Hedge, Dr. Ezra S. Gannett, John Weiss, H. M. Dexter and other clergymen. Rev. Edward Everett Hale was particularly happy in his characterization of the various pastors who had served the parish in days gone by, closing with an eloquent and heartfelt tribute to its present yet absent minister in California, Thomas Starr King. He especially deprecated the estimate of Mr. King as an orator rather than a thinker, and as a poet rather than for his manly and robust qualities. "You and I know that here is a mind of precise balance, which weighs, accepts, respects and judges, though with great rapidity, with nearly infallible decision. We know that here is a spirit utterly catholic, eager to do justice to all opinions, and untiring in its search for truth. We know that here is a heart as large as the world, so that you cannot make it understand that it should hold back from any service to be rendered to any human being. But twenty years, nay, ten, will right all this mistaken estimate."

Starr King himself wrote an admirable letter which was read at the meeting, in the course of which he said: "God means that sweeter truth shall yet bloom on the stock of the older denominations— partly by our grafting, partly by the change in the temperature of the general religious air. They have elements and energies which we have not, and possibly the great triumph of Liberal Christianity is not to come from the uprooting of any of the old structures, but from the new juices infused in their strong substance.

"Yesterday, the 31st of December, I looked out of the window on the north side of my house in San Francisco and saw buds opening in this genial climate on the flower bushes where no ray of sunshine has fallen these two months past. Liberal Christianity is part of the Divine movement to assuage the general climate of the church. Even the sects on the cold north side are bursting into bloom. There is need for us yet, as a distinctive and to some extent combative party. But our mission is to hasten the time when the church in general shall modify her creeds and grant more freedom to thought and organize more charity, and receive again into fellowship the needful forces which her narrowness has spurned."

The catholicity of Mr. King's nature is so admirably displayed in a discourse on Spiritual Christianity, delivered by him as the closing lecture of a series by eminent clergymen of Boston setting forth the creeds and aims of their respective denominations, that I cannot refrain from quoting passages from it. Dr. John W. Buckham, professor of Christian Theology at the Pacific School of Religion, in Berkeley, California, has recently declared this discourse to be one of the strongest and most eloquent of irenic sermons, and as timely to-day as when it

[98]

was first delivered. It also furnishes a characteristic illustration of Starr King as a preacher.

SPIRITUAL CHRISTIANITY

"The vital reception of Christianity in its highest power is shown in the soul's experience of the nearness and friendship of the Infinite Spirit. When a man comes to the knowledge that God is not far off, but nearer to his soul than He can be to the material world; when he learns that He is not hostile but cordial, that His frown when the heart is alien is the highest mercy and His wrath is grace; when he sees that distance from this Paternal love in the choice of evil is slavery, and wretchedness, and spiritual death, and, with a faith that purifies and justifies at once, pledges himself to the divine sanctity and compassion for all service and trust; when in the fulfilment of that great vow he lives in a deepening reverence for justice, a regard for truth that grows ever more devout, a sensitive recoil from evil, and above all a love that pours blessings and a sweet atmosphere of charity into society; when still further, feeling that God by His indwelling Spirit is the substance and support of his dearest life, the man sees the whole world illumined, so that the Eternal shines everywhere through the temporal, and nature is only the vesture or language of Spirit, and nothing is so certain as God's thought and providence in all things; and when such sense of the Infinite and such vision prompt and nourish humility and prayerfulness in the heart, and life becomes a sacrifice of thanksgiving, and a peace which death does not threaten and which sorrow cannot break broods in the sanctuaries of the soul,—then there is an echo in our century to the experience of

[99]

Paul who found the supreme privilege and bliss of his faith in Jesus in the spring which it stimulated him to make from the earth and its darkness, and the law and its bondage, into the light and the arms of Infinite Grace.

"There are very few who reach such a state as this. But we all need it to answer the end of our being, and to satisfy the deepest thirst of an awakened moral nature. We were all born from the Eternal life. And we receive our inheritance only when we begin consciously, and by consecration, to draw our innermost life from God. We feed on husks, we live in shadows, we drink from no undrainable fountains, until the immortal principle is so far stimulated by the Divine quickening, that the germ and promise of such an experience of the Infinite life and acceptance is in the soul. . . .

NO PARTICULAR DOGMAS ESSENTIAL

"Now, when we see that Spiritual Christianity is manifest in a life of freely consecrated service to the Almighty Father, whose character was revealed through Christ, and whose Spirit struggles with every soul, we must see that the quickening power of it is not indissolubly involved with any of the dogmas that divide and classify Christendom.

"We have a right to say now, in the interest of vital Christianity, that all theories of Christ's rank and office, and all catechism and creeds, are indifferent to the Spirit, so far as they belong to the speculative science of the Infinite, or to the philosophical interpretation of Scripture. This is the great question: how near is the man to the Spirit of God? how closely does the Christ he believes in bring him to the Infinite? how richly does he interpret to him the character of the Almighty—his equity, his providence, his interest in righteousness, his love? It is *working* truth, truth for redemption, truth that cleanses the passions, truth that burns the clouded conscience, truth that wrenches the cowardly will, truth that knocks at the heart with sweet and serious pleading, in which the Spirit hides. A notional Trinity or a notional Unity it cares not for, any more than it cares for your conception of how many strata are in the surface of the globe, or how the sun's light is connected with his substance.

"I do not argue that truth of creed is unimportant. I do not say that a symmetrical and pure theology, an adequate intellectual interpretation of the office of Christ and the meaning of Christianity, is not a most desirable thing. But I say that unless a man values and uses his conception of Christ, or his creed, as a medium of the Spirit, as a lens to condense the radiance of the everlasting world upon his soul, a *perfect* surface-believer is of no account. Some creeds have truth and little power; others have power and very little truth.

NO PARTICULAR INSTITUTIONS ESSENTIAL

"And now it is time to ask what relation Christianity, considered as the diffusive agency of the Divine Spirit, bears to *institutions*. Some men cannot disconnect—their theory will not allow them to disconnect—the religion of Jesus from a priestly order of men, a system of government, rituals in churches, and visible lines of division between a party with Christian badges on them, and the unregenerate mass of the world. This conception is wrought out in full proportions in the Catholic theory of a separate spiritual polity in civilization.

[101]

"When a Catholic talks with you about the Church of Christ as a social power, he means nothing more, and he cannot conceive how anything else can be meant by it, than the miraculous diffusion of Divine grace through Pope, Bishops, Decrees, Clergy, Sacraments, to those people who believe in Pope, and Clergy, and Sacraments, and who go to them regularly for help and nutriment. The visible organization of the Church is, to the devout Catholic, the immense and divine-built battery for the spiritual electricity of Heaven. And no one can receive a stream or spark of it, until he visibly joins hands with the faithful around the Altar, and obtains it from the magical touch of the Priest.

"Most of the Protestant sects, though their theories are far less imposing than this one of the Roman hierarchy, still cling to the idea—some with greater, some with less fullness of proportion in their schemes—that Christianity has some material channels which are divinely instituted (and so as precious as the religion itself) through which its saving virtue pours. The Church of Christ to them is still, in some sense, a Corporation. And a man in becoming a part of it must pass visibly, by some act or profession before men, from the side of the world where there is no grace, to the ecclesiastical side where help is ready for him, if he fulfills the conditions on which it is offered.

"Over these conceptions of Christianity must be set such an estimate of institutions as will fit the fact that the Gospel of Christ has been put into society as an all-penetrating force of social redemption. See how Jesus always interpreted the action and the future of the regenerative power concentrated in Him, through imagery drawn from the most free and diffusive energies in nature. That Spirit that vivifies the world, moves like *the wind*,—no more to be included within the boundaries of sect and sacrament, than the wind can be encompassed by cathedrals and council-domes. Again, the forces of his truth are *seeds,* scattered not over a few ecclesiastical acres, but over the field of the world, to be nourished by the unsectarian light and rain. And 'the kingdom of God is *within* you,' so that the power of it in the world is exactly equal to the truth, and the sweetness, and the aspiration, and the devotion to God and man, that hide as qualities in human bosoms, and stream as influence from them into society. Still further, 'the kingdom of heaven is like leaven which a woman took and hid in three measures of meal.' It works not from an organized, visible, and aggressive centre, but as an interpenetrating, vivifying force. You cannot mechanically separate the vitality from the dead resistance. It works by secret agency to make each particle alive, and a new germ of life.

CHRISTIANITY A SOCIAL FORCE

"The Christianity of the Spirit, therefore, is the sum of all the redeeming life-forces in our civilization. Nothing less than all the arteries of society are its ducts. Since the day of Pentecost the renovating forces of history are its vesture. Just as the quickening element of the Gospel is not dogma, and will not be imprisoned in dogma, but will look through it and stream through it even when it is unsymmetrical and ungracious,—so it is not an ecclesiastical institution, and will not be imprisoned in any or all of them. But it uses them all for its purposes:

[103]

Mediæval, Episcopal, Presbyterian, Methodist, Moravian, Congregational, Quaker, and countless other agencies besides.

"For social worship there must be, of course, some special rites, and order, and bonds; and those in which different classes of believers feel most free, and find most joy, are best for them. Yet the Spirit is not pledged to any order as a polity for Christendom. And where the most symmetrical order and liturgy become an occasion of complacency, and pride, and aristocratic schism of the heart from the community of believers, the polity is not of the spirit at all. It is an encroachment of 'this world,' an entrenchment of the 'natural man' within the area that is supposed to be especially consecrated to Christ. Apostolical succession, for instance, is no more possible as a law for the church than an equivalent theory would be in the world of art. Think of trying to institute in such a way, the right and the gift of teaching beauty! Think of a hierarchical pretension in the artistic world, claiming that only the students upon whom Raffaelle, or Michael Angelo, or Murillo, or Rubens, or Reynolds, or West, or Turner, or Allston, had laid his hands, were rightfully consecrated and equipped to paint, and to educate the taste of men! By all means have studies, and studios, and thorough intercourse with the masterpieces of ages. But leave room for genius,—its freedom, its new methods, and its fire. And do not try to conduct the potent and volatile essence of inspiration, which flows only from the laying on of God's hand, along the fixed methods of any confederation.

"The Spirit broods over *society* to vitalize it, and not exclusively over the Church. The Spirit has not shown itself partial to any organization of ecclesiasti-

[104]

cal order. It leaves the old Catholic corporation, to stimulate the world through Luther and the Reformers. And it is just as ready to break out again through the Catholic forms, and retreat from Protestant ones, when any branch of the elder Church puts itself in the condition to invite its grace, and the new Church prefers to live on memory, and begins to be proud, formal, and cruel. It delights to pour itself through preaching and the Sunday, just to the extent that the preacher has a receptive soul, and the people have hearing hearts. It streams through the holiest sacrament, and most freely when those that commune offer life as a service of thanksgiving and sacrifice to the Infinite love in the spirit of Christ, and ask for more of its breath. But we must not forget that it leaps out of a church as freely as into it. It makes a good book its channel rather than a proud bishop, though the book be written by an unprofessing layman. It discharges immeasurably more of its essence through such a novel as 'Little Dorrit' than through such volumes as Dr. Breckinridge's 'Knowledge of God Objectively Considered.' It no more acknowledges a religious newspaper as its organ than a secular one, if it is not humbly edited, and does not increase the sway of meekness and charity in those that read it, —a very severe test for many of them. It moves through all the efforts, all the eloquence, all the literature, all the homes, all the charity organizations, all the laws, all the public bounties, that are interpreting sweet and serious truth, nourishing goodness, spreading the sway of the spirit of sacrifice, banishing injustice, making the world less selfish, and more pious. For these are hastening the true Millennium, when all law, all government, all literature, all life shall be pure and reverent and charitable; and when so-

[105]

ciety shall be organized by Christ's spirit, and become the Church, and thus the whole lump be leavened.

ALL THE SECTS USEFUL

"Here, therefore, we have something to say upon the development of the life and thought of Christendom and the meaning and usefulness of sects. The Church was left unhampered by creeds from the pen of Jesus, or of Apostles, to work out its science of theology freely,—as all science is worked out through error, through cumulative effort, and through failure, —and to add to the riches of its vital literature by a manifold and ever multiplying experience. We are *in the era of the Spirit,* and the Church is to-day under the pressure and guidance of the Holy Ghost.

"Christendom is young. Look forward a hundred centuries, and see if you can imagine that the intellect of the Church will then be tethered to the metaphysics of religion shaped before modern science and philosophy and poetry were born. We cannot tell yet what the theology of Christendom is to be. The sects that have arisen thus far have each helped, through their differences, to accumulate evidence, by appearing as witnesses or counsel in the court of history for some oppressed or slighted truth.

"But the sects have done a greater service by showing us, with more and more varied and copious illustration, how deep and rich, how sweet and sublime, is Spiritual Christianity itself, when it issues in its appropriate literature of sentiment and life. Lord Bacon spoke of the ample and graceful classic mythology as the airs of earlier ages breathed into the trumpets and pipes of the Grecians. So Christianity, of which the Spirit struck the key-notes in the souls

[106]

of Apostles in Palestine, has been widening in varia-
tion and deepening in harmony with all the consecrated temperaments that have risen in the ages thus
far to articulate its airs.   We must pierce below the
creed-symbols of each party in Christian history, and
find the justification and necessity of its existence in
the fresh quality of its sentiment, or the new movement or modulation by which it has enriched the com-
pass of the symphony of grace.

CHRISTIAN LITERATURE

"Think of the range of the literature of Christian
devotedness and insight.   It runs from the 'Shepherd
of Hermas' and the prayers of the earliest liturgies,
touching different keys in different centuries and
sects, till it includes now Augustine's 'Communion
with God,' à Kempis' 'Imitation of Christ,' Tauler's
'Sermons,' the 'Meditations of Archbishop Leighton
and Bishop Hall,' Fénélon's 'Letters,' Taylor's 'Holy
Living and Dying,' Baxter's 'Saints' Rest,' Sweden-
borg's 'Divine Love and Wisdom,' Edwards' 'Sweet
Thoughts of Christ,' Wesleyan 'hymns,' Martineau's
'Endeavours after the Christian Life,' Theodore Parker's 'Ten Sermons,' and Newman on the 'Soul.'
That belongs to essential Christianity, Spiritual
Christianity, which issues in the quickening power of
these books, and gleams out in the life of all consecrated men, whether they be men of action, of suffering, or of prayer.   All are necessary to enable us to
appreciate Christianity.   For it is continually un-
folding itself in history.   And the Spirit needs every
aperture of race, and temperament, and culture, to
work out fully the mighty theme whose notes are
printed in the first Scriptures of the Church.

[107]

THE UNITY OF THE SPIRIT

"And now, if I may gather up all that I have been trying to say in a statement, let me say that only those elements of the faith and life of every church that can pass up into anthems, chants, and hymns, as an offering to the Infinite,—only those sentiments which can be set to music,—are its worthy and enduring elements. You cannot put proofs of the Trinity, or controversial supports of the Unity of God,—the logic of Bishop Bull, or the arguments of Professor Norton,— into hymns. You cannot put the difference between a feeling of the depravity of nature, and of the depravity of conduct and life, into a Psalm. When three souls feel equally the riches of Infinite love, though one receives it through a Trinitarian, another through an Arian, another through a Humanitarian dogma, you could not put their disputes about the size of the window through which they obtain their light into a chorus. You cannot chant rubrics, and the hostilities of catechisms, and thirty-nine Articles, and Canons of the Council of Trent, and damnatory clauses of the Athanasian creed.

"But reverence for God, devout prostration before the law which 'the Father' represents; penitent love answering to the pity and sacrifice which 'the Son' interprets, and devotion to humanity out of such consecration; joy in the ever-present grace, and prayer for the quickening life which 'the Spirit' symbolizes; adoration of Infinite holiness, submission to Infinite sovereignty, grateful trust in Infinite compassion,— sentiments in which, when developed free, Trinitarian and Unitarian, Calvinist and Arminian, Partialist and Universalist, come at once into fellowship, —these fly to music for expression.

[108]

"We shall drop our contentions about Trinity and Unity, about free will and constraining election, when we reach heaven. We may not understand, even to eternity, the constitution of the Infinite personality; but alienations on account of mental measurings of substantial truth will not obtain there. There will be no reverend Angels to preach on such themes as, Why am I a Calvinist, a Baptist, or an Episcopalian? But no doubt we shall still be ranged there, as here, by the sentiments to which we most naturally give utterance. And we shall see there, doubtless, what need there is of the utmost power of every party to celebrate the circle of the Divine glory; how deep is the justice, how broad the providence, how high the love, that must be acknowledged in the twined harmony of heavenly hosannas.

"Let us pray that we may yield our mind and will to the Spirit; that by its light we may see through our creeds into the all-important verities of the substantial world; that we may be in life and worship instruments of Christian music, more than soldiers of Calvinistic or Unitarian camps; and that we may be lifted, at last, by the Spirit to that world where we shall experience the truth that, 'whether there be prophecies, they shall fail; whether there be tongues, they shall cease; whether there be knowledge, it shall vanish away' before the charity that 'never faileth,' which gives the 'unity of the Spirit,' and is 'the fulfilling of the law.' "

CHAPTER VI

LECTURING ON THE PACIFIC COAST

ONE object of Mr. King's settlement in California was, as we have seen, to escape the drudgery of public lecturing. But circumstances were against him and he found himself unable to refuse the invitations which soon poured in upon him from all parts of the State. Indeed, the very week of his arrival he gave the first of a course before the Mercantile Library Association in San Francisco, consisting of lectures he had delivered at the East. In a letter to a friend he humorously refers to the opening one: "Last evening I commenced the course with 'Substance and Show,' and drew a glorious picture at the close (colored with the lecturer's genius!) of San Francisco stretched out on its desolate hills rubbing the dust out of its eyes and washing the fleas off its feet in the great Pacific basin." Delivered in the First Congregational Church, there was a great audience, and the money receipts were unprecedented. For the most part he used his existing literary material, but he wrote four or five new lectures. One of these on "Books and Reading," written in two days, was an especial favorite, and became a literary inspiration to his hearers.

Another address on "The Earth and the Mechanic

Arts" was an eloquent tribute to the dignity and importance of labor, which must have thrilled every mechanic that heard it.

Called upon to make an address at an Agricultural Fair in Stockton he acquitted himself admirably. On his return to the city he was rallied by friends on his audacity in handling such a theme, and asked what in the world he knew about farming. "Absolutely nothing!" he confessed. "Why, my people tell me I cannot even distinguish the goats from the sheep in my own congregation."

These new lectures were of a very different order from those he had delivered at the East. As a writer in the San Francisco *Evening Bulletin* tells us: "He polished his sentences less; he waited no longer on fine fancies, he dropped down to good plain talk for minutes together in his addresses; and then, when his hearers were rested, he blazed out with passages that swept away all thought but of the one subject that possessed him." Invitations to lecture poured in upon him, and soon he was busy again in his old field of labor, visiting not only the interior of the State but Oregon and Nevada as well. Everywhere he met with an appreciative hearing and became immensely popular, not only as a public speaker but for his fine personal qualities.

Curious and amusing were some of his experiences. He told with boyish glee of an enthusiastic woman who greeted him at the close of a lecture: "I'm so glad you talkative men are coming round again.

[111]

For myself, I have such a thirst for intellectooal people that I could just set and listen to lectures from now till the Fourth of July!" On another occasion he was invited to lecture before a literary society in a California mining community. Arriving early he strolled about the town, and presently came upon two red-shirted, big-booted miners who were studying a bill-board which announced that T. Starr King, of San Francisco, would lecture that evening on "Socrates and His Age." "Bill," said one of them disgustedly to his mate, "who was So-crates, and who the —— cares how old he was?"

One consequence of these lecturing tours was that he gained a large knowledge of the Pacific Coast, its scenery, resources and society.

Here Starr King was in his element. Undismayed by the hardships of travel in those early days, disregardful of discomfort and weariness, he availed himself of every opportunity to explore the marvels and witness the sublimities of the California mountains. He revelled in the sight of the imposing, snow-clad ranges of the Sierras, their gigantic chasms, foaming rivers, leaping waterfalls and crystal lakes; their virgin forests and vegetable wonders; the vast stretches of fertile prairie at their feet, waving with billowy grain, or prodigal with teeming orchards.

In the summer of 1860 Starr King visited Yosemite and the Big Trees, and his letters to the East were full of the joy of this new experience. This delight also found expression in two eloquent sermons preached to his congregation on his return to San Francisco, and later included in the volume of his printed discourses,[1] "Lessons from the Sierra Nevada," and "Living Water from Lake Tahoe." The following summer he extended his journey, punctuated with lectures, to Oregon, Washington, and British Columbia, and as far north as Nootka Sound. In a series of brilliant letters to the *Boston Evening Transcript* Starr King pictured the splendors of the Sierras, the Yosemite and the Big Trees, thus imparting to dwellers on the Atlantic seaboard their first adequate impression of the scenic wonders of the Pacific Coast, and becoming the forerunner of the gifted company of nature-writers and poets who have since eloquently described them. It was the intention of Mr. King to write some day a work on the Sierras which might be a companion volume to his book on the White Hills of New Hampshire, and he tentatively conferred with his Boston publishers on the matter.

Letters to Eastern friends communicate to them his first impressions of Nature's wonders on the Pacific Coast.

"MARIPOSA COUNTY,
"Among the California Big Trees.
"July 14, 1860.

"To *Rev. William R. Alger:*

"At your delightful home in Swampscott last Sep-

[1] "Christianity and Humanity," Boston, 1877.

[113]

tember we *talked* California, I am living it. Three days ago in San Francisco I received your genial, generous and welcome letter from the beach. And it just occurs to me that you will not object to a hurried answer on poor paper,—a mere 'pencilling by the way'—written in the most romantic part of California,—among the Sierras, amidst the Big Trees of Mariposa, and at the foot of the Monarch of the Grove.

"It is Saturday evening, 5¼ P. M. (8½ P. M. with you) and the delicious afternoon light is pouring down the snuff-colored back of the Titan over my head, who is as old at least as Christianity. I have just put a measuring line around him. His girth is ninety feet. There is another, half-decayed—all the bark having moulded, who is 100 feet and over in circuit. But the one at whose root I am scratching these words, is vigorous, and sends out green shoots a hundred feet up which are flashing in the evening splendor. There are nearly three hundred of the same species in the grove, measuring from forty to ninety feet in circumference. The bark is about twenty inches thick and very soft and delicate in texture. Its hue is one of the chief fascinations of the grove. The voices of the party—seven men— with me, sound strangely, hallowing in the distance, in this natural temple in which man is a mite. Above their noise swells the musical melancholy of these old conservatives, wakened by winds that sweep from the snow-capped granite of the Sierras which we see across a mighty gorge, by a walk of but a few rods distance. I can scarcely credit my senses that I am here, and that it will require four weeks for this to reach you. I hope it will assure you that old friends are not forgotten. I do not look

upon any strange and impressive scene without thinking of you and Hedge and Whipple, with gratitude
that I have known you, and greater gratitude that I
can love you without being forgotten.

"The Guide, who looks like Henry Ward Beecher,
and would serve as his double, asks: 'Gettin' putty
well through, mister?' I say, 'Yes,' so I must stop.
To-morrow I go to the Yosemite Notch and Falls,
the great wonder of the State.

"P. S.

"Sunday evening: In the Yosemite pass, under
rocks *five thousand* feet sheer! El Gebor!! Great
is matter and the force of cohesion! I close this note
in sight of a river which pitches 1500 feet at one leap,
and then takes two more, one 400 and the other 500,
and the roar!—"

In the following summer he writes to his parishioner and friend, R. B. Swain:

"YREKA, May 29, 1861.
"Here I am, perched on the top of the State. The
journey has been quite fatiguing. From Shasta to
Yreka we were twenty-seven hours on the road, and I
had an outside seat on the stage day and night, without a shawl. But I am all right, and my brain has
settled down again, right side up, I believe. From
Shasta town I caught the first view of Shasta Butte;
it was just after sunrise and the view was glorious
indeed. I preached after the vision for a Methodist
minister, and ought to have preached well, but am
afraid I didn't. Yesterday I devoted to the study of
Mt. Shasta. I had it in view for ten hours. It is
glorious beyond expression. It far exceeds my con-

ception of its probable grandeur. I am glad I named my book The White *Hills*. To-day is very cloudy and the mountain is shrouded to the base. The whole region is sublime."

The following summers he was permitted to behold the scenic splendors of Oregon, Washington, and the lordly Columbia River. En route he writes his friend, R. B. Swain:

"YREKA, July 21, 1862.

"It is quite hot here to-day, but as it is not 100 degrees nobody calls it hot. Anywhere in the nineties, even 99, is moderate. We rode all night of Saturday through from Shasta here, making the trip in 28 hours. The journey from here will be terribly hard, and I almost regret that I made the overland trail. From Jacksonville, where my wife and I go to-morrow, to Salem (Oregon) will be as tough as it can be —it will take three or four days. I doubt if I have time to see all I wish of Oregon and Puget Sound. It will take me another week to reach Portland, and I begin to fear I shall have to abandon the whole Puget Sound and Victoria expedition. The expenses are simply frightful. It costs me over $80 for passage from Marysville to Shasta town, and if I travel through part of Oregon by extras, as I must, $60 a day will be the lowest I can do it for, and I have purchased through tickets besides."

Every available interval of the journey was punctuated with letters to distant friends, that they might share in his delight.

LECTURING ON THE PACIFIC COAST

To *Randolph Ryer:*

"PORTLAND, OREGON, August 7, 1862.

"You see where I am. And Julia is also here. On Monday, July 14th, we took it into our heads that we would visit Oregon, Washington Territory, the British possessions, Puget Sound, and all sorts of places where hardship was to be experienced and good scenery to be found. So we started on an overland trip through Northern California, all the length of Oregon to the northern boundaries of Washington Territory and Victoria, the British city on Vancouver island. By the way we travel Victoria is about one thousand miles from San Francisco.

"Julia has borne the tremendous stretch of stageriding wonderfully well. And what scenery we have had! Mt. Shasta we have enjoyed on all sides of his mighty bulk and superb form. He is almost 15,000 feet high, and rises from a plain, draped in eternal snow. The mountains of Oregon we have passed through and had views of the wonderful line of peaks—Jefferson, the Three Sisters, Hood, Adams, St. Helens, and Rainier. And the Columbia River! It is worth a journey from New York to sail up its lordly tide and see the stupendous snow cones from its glorious level. We made a trip this week more than a hundred miles up the Columbia to the Dalles, where the whole river pours through a channel 200 feet wide. On the way what views of Hood and St. Helens! At the Dalles we saw old Hood at sunset, not more than twenty-five miles distant by air-line. He towers 14,500 feet from his base, which is much higher than Mt. Blanc from its base. Across the Columbia, in Washington Territory, Mt. Adams, but little farther off, towers nearly 14,000 feet, built up with more rugged masonry than Hood.

[117]

"Going down the Columbia we passed at one time within fifteen miles air line of Hood, and had the clearest view possible of his tremendous bulk and noble peak and blazing snow.

"But what a view of him still nearer to Portland, not far from Fort Vancouver! There he sits on a throne, above ridge after ridge of the wilderness, every particle of his height visible, and three-quarters of it covered with snow, which droops in exquisite fringes into the lower ravines. And you see him over a vast broad reach of the river itself! I do not believe the world can surpass this spectacle.

"I have lectured in Portland to a large audience on the War, and again on a rare subject: 'Substance and Show.' I shall preach here Sunday the first Unitarian sermon in these wilds. Next week for Puget Sound—then to Victoria—then home."

To *Rev. Dr. Henry W. Bellows of New York:*

"SAN FRANCISCO, August 20, 1862.
"My dear Bellows,
"I have just returned from a visit of five weeks to the great country north of us, having taken my wife under my arm and staged it overland through upper California—by the base of superb Mt. Shasta, up all Oregon, seeing majestic and magnificent Mt. Hood in all lights and framings,—beyond the Cascade Mountains on the Columbia river—across to Washington Territory and through the exquisite tangles of Puget Sound to Victoria—and thence down by sea to our metropolis again. By land thirteen hundred miles, by sea eight hundred. I have lectured a good deal, by urgent entreaty. I have preached the Liberal Christian word for the first time in Oregon and Washington, and drove the stake for a log custom-

house, with a speech, on the northernmost limit of the United States on the Straits of Fuca, near Cape Flattery. It was a glorious journey to both of us, and we return with new strength to bear the terrible strain of the military and public crisis in Virginia.

"What a proud domain is ours! The wilderness of which Bryant sung in his youth, the lovely streams and savage peaks which Irving's 'Astoria' illumined with the soft afternoon light of his genius, appropriate to the far West, are now swarming with thousands of gold-seekers and finders. Flathead Indians buy hats to fit their steep-pitched skulls from Genin's of New York, Blackfeet buy boots in forest shops from Lynn; a noble wagon-road across the Rocky Mountains connects the sources of the Columbia with navigable waters of the Missouri; and merchants of St. Louis compete with those of Portland, Oregon, in supplying the miners of our new Salmon river gold fields. The tide is setting eastward again under the Stars and Stripes, and the desolate passes of the Northern Rocky Mountains are feeling the shuttles of civilization fly with alternate beats from the Pacific Coast and the Mississippi."

CHAPTER VII

A EULOGIST OF CALIFORNIA SCENERY

THE Pacific Coast regions which Mr. King visited in those early days—only twelve years after the discovery of gold in California—have now been made accessible to hosts of sight-seers who annually visit them for health or pleasure. Their scenic wonders have been portrayed—often with great fidelity and beauty—by innumerable writers and artists. Yet the freshness and felicity with which this pioneer artist in words described the scenery of the "land of sunshine and of gold," and his power of communicating to others the impression it made on his sensitive nature, would seem to justify a selection from the score or more letters which Starr King found time to write the *Boston Evening Transcript* amidst all his absorbing labors for country and humanity.

Thus in the summer of 1860 Mr. King described the wondrous beauty of spring-time in the San Mateo, Sonoma and Santa Clara valleys. He wrote of their marvellous wealth of wild flowers, of the vast fields of poppies waving on their slender stems like the billows of an inland sea, of the vines of roses, geranium, heliotrope and fuchsia climbing to the

[120]

house-tops and embowering them with beauty and fragrance. The trees were of a different order than those at the East. Sturdy live oaks, sycamores, the locust, yew, camphor, magnolia, palmetto, myrtle, acacia in twelve varieties, pepper tree and many varieties of eucalyptus predominated. Above all, the blossoming orchards radiant with color and charm —almonds, apples, pears, cherries, oranges, apricots, peaches, plums and prunes—delighted his eyes. He dwells on the luxurious yield of berries and nuts. He tells of a golden russet apple tree, one year from the bud, with the girth of one's fore-finger and three feet high, with two dozen apples upon it. He dilates on the giant spread of grape-vines with their clusters of purple and golden fruit, and the ripening treasure of the grainfields, more precious even than that of the mines; he discourses on cattle and horses and sheep.

A newly discovered cave in El Dorado County, 160 miles away, so stirred Mr. King's mountaineering spirit that he made more than one visit to it, and described it to his Eastern audience.

Another letter is devoted to a careful study of mining in California. He gives a graphic picture of the stage ride, the pack-animals, the dreary mining villages and camps, with their shanties, saloons and billiard rooms, the "honest miner of the Far West," the prospector with pick and pan. He describes the various stages and kinds of mining—the cradle and "long tom," the sluicing, tunnelling, shafting, river fluming, gulching, crushing, and hydraulic tearing away of bluff and cañon wall, "by which the soil, the rock, the beds of powerful streams, and the hidden strain of a mountain's heart are made to yield the shining dust that was mixed with them ages ago." There are, he informs his readers, over seven thousand miles of these artificial water courses in the state to carry the indispensable flood into the heart of a thousand mining districts.

Mr. King had a quick eye for everything that was vital and characteristic of a region and its inhabitants, and burned with desire to impart his own reactions to others. Through all his communications shone the love of his early New England home, its scenery, institutions, customs, and the old-time friends from whom his new environment could not wean him. On the first of October, 1861, he writes:

"Ocean Beach, near San Francisco.

"Four days ago I drove out upon the noble beach in the rear of our city. I say the rear, for San Francisco looks inland. A long placid bay dreams at her feet. She lifts her eyes to the hills, the far-off slopes of the Sierra, 'from whence cometh her help.' They are discernible, they and the foamy whiteness on the crests of their enchanted surge, from the dimpled summit of Mt. Diablo yonder. Our city turns her face persistently towards the East—signifying that California has no insane vision of independence; that she desires no isolated sway over the Pacific, but is bound by loyalty and heart to the empire whose flag she plants on Mendocino, the Hatteras of the West,

[122]

and under which she has 'sucked of the abundance
of the seas and of treasures hidden in the sand.'
Read the figures of her recent vote and decide if I
interpret her attitude wrongly.

"As soon as our horses struck the bright sand, eight
miles from our door, my companion exclaimed:
'There is nothing like sea air. This is Rockport
over again.' We can show you no such luxury of
woods as you on Cape Ann can revel in—those
thickets of Pigeon Cove in which one loses the belief
that he is within a hundred miles of the surf, except
that now and then a subtone of tender thunder rolls
in beneath the rustle of birches, or a sudden rift in
the foliage reveals the blazing blue of the sea united
by creeping, creamy foam with the curved and flashing gray of 'Coffin's Beach.' Ah, those winding
subtle aisles in which you all but needed the thread
of Ariadne, opening now upon a patch of swamp,
aflame with the cardinal flower, now upon hedges
laden with quarts of blackberries, and now into sombre shades of pine where no secular thoughts can
thrive! No, we cannot show you in the neighborhood of our beach here, such wood paths or such
foliage. Flowers we revel in. They will grow with
us out of the sunshine, in the sand, within the very
spray of the breakers. But trees we cannot offer
you. We go to the Sierra, plunge into the glories
of their forests, and come back to live a year on the
remembrance, and to wonder how the flowers and
vines consent to bloom so luxuriously without the
fellowship of their strong and stately brethren.
Neither can we compete, on our beach, with your
Rockport waves. Not because ours is the Pacific
Sea. We know how to be sublime with our billows
as well as the hoarse Atlantic. But no beach can

show such billows as glorify a shelving rocky shore after a storm. Beach-waves are thin and rhetorical contrasted with the chasing rock-waves, which are heavy, impassioned, Websterian. Vividly I recall the joy of watching the compact battalions of the ground swell after a storm that had stirred the hiding places of the ocean's might. I have seen Niagara in winter; but the gathering of one of these billows a quarter of a mile long, in a smooth grey sea, towering and darkening as it rides on, setting free a gleam of brilliance here and there from its threatening and thinning edge, and then pouring a long avalanche of light—the thunder and the flash at the same instant— up the slope of granite that allows no stain to the emerald loop or the creamy dash of the surge—this is grander than Niagara; and whoever can see this, as Pigeon Cove shows it once or twice in the summer, needs not to envy the sight-seeing even of angels.

"But on our Pacific Ocean Beach we can beat you in some things. You can see nothing on your rocks and near them, but a few quails, and here and there some sand-birds and plover, with now and then a timid mink startled by the bathers. We can show you cranes as tall as the President of the United States, and eagles screaming over the waves, as our national eagle hovers over the moral wave from Nebraska to Aroostook, and on an island a little way from shore, a school of immense sea-lions climbing the rocks as well as they can without feet, and barking in a hoarse chorus either of joy or defiance. Choose a day that is transparent and you will see the rocks called the Farralones, twenty-three miles out from the Golden Gate. There are six of them, and Sir Francis Drake put them into English literature forty years before Plymouth Rock was touched by a

Pilgrim foot. The largest of them is a jagged boulder nearly a mile long, without a tree or shrub, but carpeted every June with green spotted with brown, not exactly in the form of lichens, but in the shape of eggs, which find their way by myriads to our markets, much to the amazement and disgust, no doubt, of the birds whose hopes of posterity are thus nipped, and who would delight to see our marauding city 'shelled' in another way. We would show you on this rock a Yankee trick, too, by which old Neptune is made to give warning to sailors of the traps he has laid for them. It is a powerful fog whistle, erected over a subterranean passage and blown by the sea which breaks into it beneath. For more than twenty hours in the twenty-four, the surf thus sounds its own alarm for a distance of seven or eight miles."

In December (31st), 1861, Starr King sent a graphic account to the *Transcript* of the unprecedented, widely-extended and disastrous floods of that winter in the interior of Central California. A district as large as the State of Massachusetts was under water. On a personal visit he found that every street in the capital, Sacramento, was inundated, in some of them the racing tides were from ten to eighteen feet deep. Stockton, Marysville, were similarly inundated. The whole district was an inland lake as big as Ontario. The loss of property, cattle and crops was immense. One third of the taxable values of the State were destroyed. There was much suffering, and on his return Mr. King actively concerned himself with the work of relief and aid.

[125]

THOMAS STARR KING

The inveterate mountain climber next essays the nearest accessible peak, the one which overlooks San Francisco Bay and was daily visible from his window.

A TRIP TO MONTE DIABLO

"There are two ways of going to Monte Diablo from this city. We can cross the bay, seven miles, by ferry, to Oakland, mount the ridge, some 1500 feet high, back of whose long wall we see the shoulders and crown of our Eminence soaring, and may drive down the further slope, through exquisite cañons and plains, green now in the glory of spring, to the very base of the monarch of our neighborhood. This would be to make a 'bee line' for our destination. Or we can travel most of the distance on a round about track by water. Let us try the latter method. We start in a little steamboat at eleven in the forenoon, thus enabling us to reach the base of the mountain before sunset. In a small, slow boat, with the tides against us, we have ample opportunity to study and enjoy the scenery around the bay. We have passed the swell of the Golden Gate and are seeing Alcatraz island grow dim behind us. On our left, as we steam up the bay, is Tamalpais, our jewel. One of these days I hope to scale it and send you a report of the splendid waterscape it commands. For on one side the ocean chafes its rugged outworks; on the other side its cañons subside into gentle slopes that are tenderly bathed by the pulsations of the Bay. The mountain rises nearly 3000 feet above the sea and supports a noble peak. But its sides are torn with such channels as we seldom see in the New Hampshire heights. In studying this hill your eyes must get used to wrinkles that would crimp Mt. Washington so that his best friends would not know him. What would I not give for a picture of Tamalpais at five in the afternoon, when the soft light falls upon the tops of those billowy ravines whose deeps of green are dimly detected through azure mist, while the shadow of the whole mountain is beginning to steal out upon the sheltered cove of San Rafael.

"Up now through the wide ring of San Pablo bay and then into the narrow straits of Carquinez we sail under the brilliant noon, and watching with delight the soft swells of unruffled green on either bank. Not a stone mars the monotonous luxury of verdure. We are approaching Benicia. But let us watch for the first appearance of Monte Diablo. From San Francisco we can see only his dome rising back of a long range of lower and nearer hills. We have turned now the flank of that range, and in a few minutes shall see him start out from base to summit. Ah, the view begins. We catch sight of the plain on which he rests. It ripples gently from the bay into the interior, then comes an encircling outwork of plateau, whose embankment is cut freely into ravines, and then the climbing line of the mountain up to a height of nearly 3000 feet, when it begins to dip again, yet not far; again it rises and springs to a second summit, the true peak, nearly 4000 feet above the water, whose smoothness we are cutting in our haste to reach the pier at Benicia.

"In half an hour we will try the ferry across to Martinez on the other side of the strait, but not till the expected rain has come. In a black volume of wrath it rolls towards us from the West, as though it would discharge in frightful thunder. But not a flash leaps from it, not a roar bursts from its wild

[127]

breast. All the rains of the Coast region are tame. I have never seen a flame of lightning, nor heard a thunder peal in this state, save on the 22nd of December, 1860. Then in San Francisco the heavens gave us some martial music. Perhaps as the rebellion was then getting under headway, and we were in danger here, it was a reveille for the Northern and Pilgrim spirit in our city and state. If so, the result must seem satisfactory. Through the roses of Martinez, and out over the green and charming plains we drive towards Clayton at the base of Monte Diablo, where the discovery of some coal mines—a great blessing to a state whose coal, via Cape Horn, is worth twenty-four dollars a ton—has started a little village and a tolerable hotel. It is fourteen miles from Martinez to our destination. We left San Francisco at eleven o'clock A. M.; we reached Clayton at 6 P. M. and are in doubt in this delicious evening air, and amid the soft and finished landscape, if we have not been driven by some beneficent sorcery into an enchanted land.

"What gracefully moulded hills! What loveliness of dimples and shadows! What an exquisite tint of green, lighter and livelier than Nature wears in New England! What stripes and patches of flowers upon the slopes! What nobleness of trees flinging their shadows singly upon an acre of unbroken beauty of grain, or entangling them as they fall from parks that are disturbed by no underbrush. Only a few months has this Clayton been in existence, and it is embosomed in a landscape which seems to have been under a line of landscape gardeners for half a dozen centuries, and over all the top of Diablo is burning with the Tyrian fire of evening. What peace, what bounty, what luxury of slope and verdure! A party

[128]

of wise, hospitable and delightful men, who are making the Geological Survey for the State, are encamped in a field nearby. Their camp fire begins to burn soon after the evening star is out. We stretch out with them on the grass near that blaze, and with a great content amid so much beauty and such rich hope for the morrow, enjoying wit and Whitney and wisdom till midnight warns us to rest.

THE ASCENT OF MONTE DIABLO

"After enjoying the untiring sweetness of the landscape around Clayton in the morning light, we join the party for the ascent of Mt. Diablo. How clear the air is! Not a wisp of vapor rests on the summit. It invites us up to a view as wide as its namesake once revealed from a Syrian peak. The distance is eight miles. You can ride on a horse or a mule, unless you prefer better company on foot. I advise you not to ride. Keep near Professor Whitney and learn the age of those steep metamorphic rocks that cast ragged and wild shadows down into the Western ravines. You won't be bored with lectures. You will get the truth in flashes, like light leaping from a burnished sabre; and in a moment after a generalization that opens a gleam for you back to pre-adamite years, back to the pulpy babyhood of Diablo, look out for a pun that would make Tom Hood envious, or a stroke of wit that would do honor to Hosea Biglow.

"And do not lag behind Professor Brewer either. You will need all the suppleness of limb which a Mount Washington experience has developed to keep pace with him. But how can you else get 'posted' in the strange botany of the upward track? He is our California Solomon. He will tell you the name of every shrub along the first three miles of our rolling

[129]

and gently rising road. He will tell you how few of them have any representatives East. What do you think of alders that are not bush but trees one hundred feet tall? What do you think of patches all aflame with scarlet larkspur, and open acres glowing with the orange splendor of squadrons of the Esch-Scholtzia, while other acres are bedecked with the nodding grace of the

'Columbine with horn of honey?'

But harder climbing begins, and as we are shut in by the walls of a ravine and lose the breeze, the heat increases.

"But the study of the formation of the mountain and the grandeur of the rocks, once fused by fire, which are adorned on the opposite wall with a few stripes of green, but with the most fantastic ribands of shadow, and the occasional gleam of the distant country, and the bright talk of the professors make the path seem short. At last we emerge from the cañon and stand out on the ridge which leads to the mountain crest. What splendor breaks upon us from the valleys at the Southeast and South! It seems to me that the word green was never understood until I looked down into the valleys of Pacheco, and Amador, and San Ramon. There was no deep, strong summer verdure like that of New England grass in July, but a rolling immensity of light-lined, flashing green. Miles and miles of slope and plain were alive with such tints as break through the foam of a clean sea-wave, when it combs upon a shelving rocky shore. The spring green on the low hills and upon the ranches between Diablo and the Coast Range has a light, cheery, gay, flashing quality which no landscape at the East ever wears. In four weeks from the

[130]

time when our party saw it, it would be a monotonous brown. Nature atones by the splendor for the brevity.

"And now we must make a strong pull for the mountain top. But don't let your enthusiasm over that green in the valleys swamp your prudence. Look out how you swing your arms carelessly among these shrubs with dark green crimped and sherry leaves—especially if your gloves are off. That is the 'poison oak,' as it is absurdly named. If it grew only on Diablo we might think that Satan had mixed its juices; but as it abounds throughout California, we will refrain from a theory which attributes to his Duskyship so wide a jurisdiction in these parts. Many persons cannot breathe the air where it grows without suffering seriously. Admire its color, converse with Professor Brewer about the probable cause of its antipathy to our race, but keep clear of it as if each of its glossy twigs warned you by a rattle.

"We have came to the last ascent. In two minutes we gain the bald crown of Diablo. No near mountains impede our vision. We turn slowly round and sweep an immense horizon. And what a spectacle! We stand 3881 feet (so Professor Whitney determined by careful calculations made during this excursion) above the Pacific—and there is its level azure on the West. We look off over the Contra Costa heights down upon the bay of San Francisco, and out through the cleft of the Golden Gate, out upon the sleeping sea to the misty blending of its blue with the calmer sky. The sleeping sea, I say. It is really roughened by a very strong breeze—for the fog is moving in shreds along the bay, and we know that a high wind is rioting over San Francisco, wild from the coolness of the ocean. But we are thirty miles from the Golden Gate by air line. The tops of the streets of San Francisco, here and there, are visible, and their sandy stripes down to the bay. The whole extent of the bay itself, whose shore line turning at right angles about midway, runs up towards the centre of the State, and measures more than a hundred miles before it begins to return, lies below us. Tamalpais lifts its sculptured gracefulness directly on the West, and combines with the long line of the Coast Range, of which he is the proudest pillar, to prevent a view of the sea-expanse beyond. Below the southerly limit of the bay we see the noble Bache mountain, named in honor of the accomplished chief of the Coast Survey, which overtops the region of the Almaden quick-silver mines.

"Turning now to the north we see above the glorious Napa valley, and forty miles away, the pyramid of Mt. St. Helena, twelve hundred feet higher than we stand. Beyond that is the Sulphur Peak that gazes down on one side upon the exquisite Russian River verdure and fertility, and on another into the streams and desolation of the Geyser Cañon. Still farther back, and thirty miles more distant, are the rocky ridges that wall the Clear Lake region, one or two of them seven thousand feet high, tipped with snow.

"Directly beneath us are the two great rivers of Central California, the Sacramento and the San Joaquin. Far up to the north, for scores of miles, we follow the receding amber of the Sacramento's tide, branching off into its tributaries. Far to the south we trace the same line of the San Joaquin through plains as bountiful as this earth upholds on her liberal bosom. But nowhere do we see a stripe of pure color in these tides. Far as we can trace them they are turbid with the burden of the washings for gold in the interior,—the mountains they are moving into the Bay of San Francisco and the sea.

"It takes some time to become accustomed to the immense scale of these plains. Out of the smooth exposure, ninety miles by air-line on the north, the beautiful Yuba Buttes leave their outline, and still the plains stretch far beyond them. It seems as if half the world might be fed by the opulence of these prairies fitly tilled.

"But what guards them on the east? Look at the magnificent barrier; what majesty, what splendor! There you see the wonderful wall of the Sierra, its foothills that roll in huge surges, all reduced by distance to regular slopes of unbroken bulwark. For two hundred and fifty miles the mighty breastwork is in view, and along the whole line crowned with blazing snow! Here and there peaks rise above it, from eleven thousand to fourteen thousand feet in height—but they do not break the impression upon the eye of an impassable wall, an everlasting prohibition by the Creator of all intercourse with the world beyond. And yet there are half a dozen passes over that embankment into Washoe, by which a light Concord wagon can travel; and the scream of the steam whistle of the Pacific Railroad will startle those icy heights before many years. As I write these very words tidings have come by telegraph, whose slender wire crosses these white solitudes, that 'President Lincoln has signed the Pacific Railroad bill.'

"Nowhere in Europe can such a vast mountain line be seen as Diablo showed us on that clear day. And what a vast extent of territory! Our scientific

[133]

companions of the Survey by their instruments and sober reckoning discovered that within the range of our vision lay an expanse of 46,000 square miles! An area as large as the State of New York! And this but little more than a quarter of California. Imagine what the state will be when all its varied mineral veins are pouring out their riches of copper and iron and coal, and silver, quicksilver and gold, and when its plains with their grain and cattle, and its foothills with their vines and orchards, are competing with its mines in the supply of plenty and wealth."

A vacation trip among the Sierras the very first summer after Mr. King's arrival in California revealed to him the splendors of their scenery, and impelled him to make their characteristic features known to the dwellers on the Atlantic side of the Continent.

AMONG THE BIG TREES

"November, 1860.

"We were very tired when we dismounted at Clarke's log hut and canvas dining tent in the glorious forest, thirty miles from Mariposa. Tired in body and in brain,—tired by our seven hours of horseback riding, and by the perpetual feast of floral beauty and sugar pine magnificence which had delighted eye and heart. But it did not take long to restore us. We were only five miles from the Mammoth Trees. An easy upland ride of an hour would lead us to the grove where the vegetable Titans we had so often read about, with a wonder tinged with unbelief, held their solemn court. . . .

[134]

"There are two large groves of the mammoth trees in California. The one which is usually visited is in Calaveras County. It contains hardly a third as many trees as the Mariposa cluster which we are in search of, but is much more easy of access. It covers about as much space as the Boston Common and a good carriage road leads to the heart of it. You drive up to a hotel and find the grounds trimmed up and the trees named and labelled for guests. The 'Hercules' in this group is 93 feet in circumference. The 'California,' 73 feet in circuit, shoots up straight as an arrow 310 feet. The 'Mother of the Forest' is 327 feet high and nearly 80 feet girth.

"The Mariposa group stands as the Creator has fashioned it, unprofaned except by fire, which long before the advent of Saxon white men, had charred the base of the larger portion of the stalwart trees. We rode on for an hour, till we reached a forest plateau five thousand feet above the sea. This, in New England, is the height of Mt. Madison, where not a thing can grow. Riding on a few rods through ordinary evergreens with dark stems, we at last catch a glimpse of a strange color in the forest. It is a tree in the distance of a light cinnamon hue. We ride nearer and nearer, seeing others of the same complexion starting out in most impressive contrast with the sombre columns of the wilderness. We are now in the grove of the Titans. The bark has a right leonine effect on the eye. We single out one of them for a first acquaintance, and dismount at its root.

"I must confess that my own feeling, as I first scanned it, and let the eye roam up its tawny pillar, was one of intense disappointment. But then, I said to myself, this is doubtless one of the striplings of the Anak brood—only a small affair of some forty feet in girth. I took out the measuring line, fastened it to the trunk with a knife, and walked around, unwinding as I went. The line was seventy-five feet long. I came to the end of the line before completing the circuit. Nine feet more were needed. I had dismounted before a structure 84 feet in circumference and nearly 300 feet high. It did not look to me twice as large as the Big Elm in Boston Common, although that is only 18 feet in circumference, and this was 28 feet in diameter.

"There are nearly three times as many of the giant species in this grove as in the Calaveras cluster. Divided into two groups, there are six hundred and fifty of them, within a space of one mile by three-quarters, one of 102 feet girth, two of 100, one of 97, and so on. More than a hundred trees measure 50 feet and upwards in circumference.

"This crowd of majestic forms explains the disappointment in first entering the grove. The general scale is too immense. Half a dozen of the largest trees, spaced half a mile apart, and properly set off by the trees of six and eight feet in girth would shake the most volatile mind with awe. Four days afterwards, on the homeward path by another trail, I struck off the track to see some big trees near Crane's Flat. The first one we approached was the only one of the species in the range of vision, and reared its snuff-colored column among some ordinary firs. How majestic it swelled and towered! My companion and I both exclaimed, 'This is the largest tree we have yet seen; this will measure more than a hundred feet in girth.' We gazed for a long time at its soaring stem, from which, a hundred feet above us, the branches that shot out bent suddenly upwards, like the pictures of the golden candlesticks in the

Hebrew temple. It seemed profane to put a measuring tape upon such a piece of organized sublimity. But we made the trial. It was just fifty-six feet in circuit—but little more than half the size of the Monarchs in Mariposa which it seemed to excel so much in majesty. There were a hundred trees in the Mariposa grove larger than this, and all of them together did not make half the impression on me that this one stamped into the brain at first sight. We need to see the 'Mother of the Forest,' for instance, towering near Trinity Church in New York, and overtopping its spire with a column whose life is older than the doctrine of the Trinity, to appreciate its vastness.

"We ought to be able to see the 'Fountain Tree' of the Mariposa Grove, a hundred and two feet in circuit, rising near the Bunker Hill Monument, and bearing up its crown eighty feet above it, to feel the marvel of its bulk and vitality. Think of that monument as a living structure. Conceive it as having grown from a granite seed whose outpouring life absorbed from the earth, and attracted from the winds fine granite dust, to be slowly compacted by internal and unerring masonry into the solid squares of its strength and its tapering symmetry! A work far more marvelous than this has been wrought by each fragment of a cone that took root 5,000 feet on a ridge of the Sierras centuries ago and now is represented by an organism of thirty feet diameter. Indeed, it is quite probable that there have been a few trees in both the Mariposa and Calaveras Groves, which have built their sublime columns out of the air through the energy of a single seed, in whose trunk Bunker Hill Monument could have been inserted and hidden, while the stem would still spring more than 200 feet above its apex stone.

[137]

THOMAS STARR KING

"What an afternoon I passed in the Mariposa Grove! I lay for half an hour alone at the root of the most colossal bole—my companions out of sight and hearing—and watched the golden sunshine mounting the amber trunk, and at last leaving a hundred feet of it in shadow to flood its mighty boughs and locks with tender luster. What silence and what mystery! How many centuries of summers has such evening splendor burnished thus the summit of its completed shaft? How long since the quickening sunbeam fell upon the first spear of green in which the prophecy of the superb obelisk was enfolded? Why cannot the dumb column now be confidential? There comes a breath of wind cooled by the snow on higher swells of the Sierras, which can be seen from the western edge of the grove;—why will not the old patriarch take advantage of that ripple through his leaves and whisper to me his age? Are you as old as Noah? Do you span the centuries as far as Moses? Can you remember the time of Solomon? Were you planted before the seed of Rome took root in Italy? At any rate tell me whether or not your birth belongs to the Christian centuries, whether we must write B. C. or A. D. against your infancy? I promised the stalwart greybeard I would tell nobody, or at most only *The Transcript,* if he would just drop into my ear the hour of his nativity. Perhaps he would have told me, if my party had not returned to disturb the conditions of a communication.

"A genial evening of life to the Methuselahs of the wilderness who were babes a thousand years ago!" [1]

[1] Prof. Willis L. Jepson, an authority on this subject, and connected with the botanical department of The University of California, informs

A EULOGIST OF CALIFORNIA SCENERY

A final selection shall be taken from Mr. King's letters describing the Yosemite Valley.

THE APPROACH TO THE YOSEMITE

"November, 1860.

"After four hours of moderate climbing through the glorious woods we began to be on the watch for some signs of the rocks that wall in the Yosemite Valley. We rode on and on, and yet saw no line ahead of a rocky activity. Our guides from Coulterville had never been over this Mariposa trail, and I began to feel almost sure that we had missed the track. Just when I was about to call a Council of War we passed out from among the stripling trees and found ourselves—on the edge of a trench in the Sierras four thousand feet deep and six or eight miles long! We came to a precipice of sheer rock which is 2700 feet deep. Immediately opposite, about a mile across, a portion of that northerly wall stands up 3800 feet high. It does not abate a jot from the perpendicular. It is clean, naked granite. A plummet could be dropped straight from its pediment to its base. On our southerly side the wall rises gradually in height to the right hand, or east, of us, and in some portions rears a spire 1600 feet higher than where we are. The great dome of smooth unspotted rock, eight miles distant from us by air-line on this southerly wall, lacks in few yards only, by measurement, of five thousand

the author: "The living Sequoia giganteas commonly range in age from 1100 to 1400 years, while a good many go to 2200 years, and one tree whose age has been determined very carefully reached 3248 years, a figure which is accurate in the sense that the range of error is limited to six or ten years either way. Figures for greater ages often published, are not the results of accurate studies."

[139]

feet above the stream that winds beneath it. But it is everywhere abrupt and sheer.

"How can I express the awe and joy that were blended and continually struggling with each other, during the half hour in the hot noon that we remained on the edge of the abyss, where the grandeurs of the Yosemite were first revealed to us? The ramparts of the vast trench curve so much that we could not see more than half its length towards the east. At our left, on the west, the course of the beautiful Merced could be followed for a dozen miles. There was a grave cheerfulness in the general aspect of the tremendous furrow, in spite of the bareness of the scraped wall, and the desolation enthroned upon the lofty summit springing 300 feet higher into the bleak air from the most northerly portion of the opposite battlement.

"I had read in a volume of travels among the highest Himalayas of the singularly blue tone of the cliffs and rocks. This was very striking in the first sight of the Yosemite. There was a delicate and most charming blue tint spread over the walls and heights. Look steadily at a cliff and it would wear a deathly ash color; a lambent light, vivifying it to the general glance. Then at the bottom, you gazed not upon desolation but upon the loveliest meadows skirted by stately trees and veined by a river as large as the upper Connecticut. On the ramparts opposite streams were plunging with reckless fury to the valley below. To our eyes, however, there was no fury:

'But like a downward smoke the slender stream
Along the cliff to fall and pause did seem.'

There was the murmur of a heavy waterfall beneath us. A slight change in our position showed us a sudden sag of the rock line on our southerly wall, and there, 1500 feet below us, a cataract which took one plunge of nearly a thousand feet before its spray was shattered on the rocks. The scene was sublime, but it was not lonely, desolate, or sombre, as I had expected. And all the angularity and hardness of line in the ramparts was soothed by some indefinable mystic grace. I was not surprised, therefore, to learn that this spot where this magnificence first bursts into vision is named Inspiration Point.

THE YOSEMITE VALLEY.

"The Yosemite valley is a pass about ten miles long, which at its eastern extremity, splits into three narrow notches, each of which extends several miles, winding by the wildest paths into the heart of the Sierra Nevada chain. For seven miles of the main valley, which varies in width from three-quarters of a mile to a mile and a half, the walls are from two thousand to nearly five thousand feet above the road and are nearly perpendicular. The valley is of such irregular width and bends so much, and often so abruptly that there is a great variety and frequent surprise in the forms and combinations of the overhanging rocks, as one rides along the banks of the stream. The patches of luxuriant meadow with their dazzling green, and the grouping of the superb firs, two hundred feet high, that skirt them, and that shoot above the stout and graceful oaks and sycamores, are delightful nests of sweetness and beauty amid the threatening awfulness—like the threads and flashes of melody that relieve the towering masses of Beethoven's harmony. The Ninth Symphony is the Yosemite of music. The Merced, which flows through the main aisle we are speaking of, is a noble stream a hundred feet wide and ten feet deep. It is formed chiefly by the streams that leap and rush through the narrow notches above referred to, and it is swollen also by the bounty of the marvellous waterfalls that pour down the ramparts of the wider valley.

"Now let us descend from Inspiration Point by a very steep trail to the level of the Merced, and ride up between the cliffs to such rude hospitality as the isolation of the region may afford. At the foot of the break-neck declivity we reach the banks of the Merced and every rod of the six miles ride to the 'hotel' awakens wonder, awe, and a solemn joy. First, we come within the sound of a sweet and steady thunder which seems to pour from heights at our right hand. Soon we ford and cross in turn a dozen rivulets that flow merrily athwart the trail, and then through a wider opening among the trees we see the parent stream. But it is no prosaic water. It is a gush of splendor, a column of concentrated light from heaven; of course, we turn our horses' heads straight toward it. Soon we dismount, and clamber over the boulders and debris around which its dishevelled strands are briskly leaping. The rich bass deepens as we rise, and before long we are in a cloud of spray that mounts

'And thence again
Returns in an unceasing shower, which round
With its unemptied cloud of gentle rain,
Is an eternal April to the ground,
Making it all one emerald.'

"Not a very 'gentle' rain, however, as our soaked clothes soon attested. I did not stay long amid the glories of its flashing iridescence, for I wished to stand by the wall itself and look up. So I pushed ahead through the blowing rainbows, and soon reached the smooth-faced ramparts. I was now entirely safe from the spray, which fell forty feet in front of me upon the boulders, and I could look up steadily, with no mist in the eyes, except what the wonder of the picture stimulated. The wall is here about a thousand feet high. It sags in the centre, and there, eight hundred feet over my head, was the curve of the cataract, as it pours from the level stream for its unbroken descent of a sixth of a mile. Not a single projection from the wall, or bulge in it, is there to fret or mar the majesty and freedom of the current. It was probably fifteen feet wide where it started in its descent. It kept its curve and a concentrated life for some 300 feet; and then gravitation got hold of it, shook it apart, and made it tumble through the air for five hundred feet more, scattering millions of pearls, and whole sheets of filmy mist, to be smitten with splendor by the sun.

"This cascade is called 'The Bridal Veil.' A worse name might be given it, but it seems to be pleading with us that 'Bridal Veil' folly might be thrown aside, and that it might be known forever by its Indian baptism 'Pohono.' Thus before we had been in the Valley twenty minutes we were at the foot of a fall as high and more beautiful than the celebrated Staubbach, the highest in Europe.

"Still we have five miles of horseback riding to the hotel. Is there such a ride possible in any other part of the planet? Nowhere among the Alps, and in no cañon of the mighty Oregon range, is there such stupendous rock-scenery as the traveller here lifts his eyes to. The Sierra Nevada has very few

[143]

peaks which make the impression which fourteen thousand feet of height ought to leave on the mind. But it may challenge any portion of the globe, except the awful gorges of the Himalaya through which the gloomy Sutlej pours, to rival the savageness and sublimity of these bluffs and spires. The Saguenay river shores are the best suggestion of the rocky sides of the Yosemite valley; but their grandest headlands are not half so high as portions of these battlements.

"After leaving the nook in which the Pohono tumbles, we found ourselves soon under a cliff twice as high. We were obliged to turn our heads back to see its crest, two thousand feet of sheer height above us. The first view was so terrible that I supposed this must be the most striking scenery in all the valley, and I was greatly astonished to learn the absolute measurement of the precipice. Opposite this cliff, on the left or northerly bank of the river, stood the sublime rock 'El Capitan,' or the 'The Chieftain.' This wonderful piece of natural masonry stands at an angle with the valley, presenting a sharp edge and two sides in one view, and how high? 3817 feet! It stands straight. There is no lazy curve-line, as in the sides of the White Mountain Notch. In fact, the monstrous mass beetles a little. You can stand on the summit and drop a plumb line to the base. I called it just now a piece of natural masonry; but the word is inaccurate. The immense escarpment has no crack or mark of stratification. It is one block of naked granite pushed up from below. On one face the wall is weather-stained, or lichen-stained with rich cream colored patches, on the other side it is ashy grey. A more majestic object than this rock I ex-

[144]

pect never to see on this planet. Great is granite, and the Yosemite is its prophet!

"On the right bank of the river, further on, we find another portion of the wall over our heads on the right hand from which two immense obelisks are upreared. They are called 'The Sisters.' Bah! These 'Sisters' look down upon you from an altitude of 3500 feet, and occasionally send their respects to the meadow in a flake or two of a thousand tons, dropping perpendicularly more than half a mile. Another mile and we are under the shadow of 'The Sentinel.' Look up at that 'pinnacled silence'! There is a height greater than the twin obelisks we last left, and even overlooking by 500 feet the wall El Capitan on the opposite bank below. How charmingly the frosts have gnawed and ravaged its upper edges! We ride close to the base, hold our heads back, and gaze long at the delicate points and lines of those splinters in the zenith. The highest of these needles is 4347 feet over our heads. Reader, do you appreciate that height? Probably you have been in 'The Glen' among the White Mountains, and you remember the sharp peak of Mt. Adams, whose pyramid is so symmetrical, seen from the porch of the Glen House. Imagine Mt. Adams cloven by Omnipotence midway from its apex to its lowest stone, so that you could ride on horseback within a few rods of the smooth wall, and look up from plinth to crown! But that summit is not quite 4300 feet above the glen; and you can now judge what it is to turn your eyes to the dim turrets of 'The Sentinel' in Yosemite!

"The wall opposite the Sentinel has a height at one point of 4480 feet. The valley here is about a mile wide. If its two sides could be pried from

[145]

their foundations and tipped towards each other, they could not fall. They would meet and support each other and convert the valley into a mighty cave, with a roofing more than three-quarters of a mile high. In fact, early in the summer afternoon, the opposite wall is in gloom, and throws its immense shadow athwart the meadows beneath, robbing them of four hours of sunshine which the fields under the Sentinel enjoy. These shadows engage our attention, with the continuous line of rampart under which we ride still three miles before reaching our goal. And the hotel is not the end of the valley, or of its wonders. Still beyond as we catch sight of it are two immense domes of bare and glistening granite. How high are they? What is the measure of that southerly one which the declining sun is sheathing with impalpable gold? If it were 23 feet higher it would be 5000 feet. As it stands it is 300 feet taller than Mt. Washington in the White Hills from the points nearest its base, while the side of St. Peter's is not more perpendicular than the wall which it crowns.

"But as we approach the hotel and turn towards the opposite bank of the river, what is that

'Which ever sounds and shines
A pillar of white light upon the wall
Of purple cliffs aloof descried?'

That is the highest waterfall in the world, the Yosemite cataract, 2500 feet in its plunge, dashing from a break or depression in a cliff 3200 feet sheer! Mr. Greeley in his account of his very hurried visit to the valley a year ago (in September, 1859), calls it a mere tape-line of water dropped from the sky. Perhaps it is so toward the close of the dry season, but as we saw it, the blended majesty and beauty of it, apart from the general sublimities of the Yosemite gorge, would repay a journey of a thousand miles. There was no deficiency of water. It was a powerful stream 35 feet broad, fresh from the Nevada, that made the plunge from the brow of the awful precipice; and our resting place on the southerly bank of the Merced, in the pass, afforded us a most favorable angle for enjoying its exhaustless charm.

> 'Like sheet-lightning,
> Ever brightening,
> With a low melodious thunder,
> All day and all night it is ever drawn
> From the brain of the purple mountain,
> Which stands in the distance yonder.'

"The thunder, however, though certainly melodious, is by no means low, as may be imagined when the measure of the fall is reported. At the first leap it clears 1497 feet; then it tumbles down a series of steep stairways 402 feet, and then makes a jump to the meadows 518 feet more. The three pitches are in full view, making a fall of more than 2400 feet.

"But it is the upper and highest cataract that is the most wonderful to the eye, as well as most musical. The cliff is so sheer that there is no break in the body of water during the whole of its descent of more than a quarter of a mile. It pours in a curve from the summit, fifteen hundred feet to the basin that hoards it but for a moment for the cascades that follow. And what endless complexities and opulence of beauty in the forms and motions of the cataract! Comparatively narrow at the top of the precipice, it

[147]

widens as it descends, and curves a little on one side as it widens, so that it shapes itself, before it reaches its first bowl of granite, to the figure of the comet that glowed in our skies two years ago. More beautiful than the comet, however, we can see the substance of this watery loveliness ever renew itself, and ever pour itself away. Our readers have seen the splendid rockets that on Fourth of July nights burst into serpents of fire. This cataract seems to shoot out a thousand serpentine heads or knots of water which wriggle down deliberately through the air, and expend themselves in mist before half the descent is over. Then a new set bursts from the body and sides of the fall, with the same fortune, and thus the most charming fret-work of watery nodules, each trailing its vapory train for a hundred feet, or more, is woven all over the cascade, which swings, now and then, thirty feet each way on the mountain side, as if it were a pendulum of watery lace. Once in a while, too, the wind manages to get back of the fall, between it and the cliff, and then it will whirl it round and round for two or three hundred feet, as if it were determined to wring it dry. We could lie for hours, never tired of gazing at this cataract, but ever hungry for more of the witcheries of motion and grace that refine and soften its grandeur."

It should be borne in mind in reading these descriptions of California scenery by Starr King that they were not the deliberate, carefully worded studies of a nature-writer, but the hastily recorded impressions of a vacation tourist.

The series ends with a vivid description of Mr. King's exploration of the upper ravines of the Yo-

[148]

MOUNT STARR KING, YOSEMITE, SIERRA NEVADA

PHOTO BY FISKE

semite Valley, not then as accessible as now. The South Dome, Royal Arches, Mirror Lake, and other scenic features receive due mention. Thence he "climbed above the Vernal Fall, where the Merced River pours from a perpendicular granite rampart 500 feet; and back of this, half a mile distant, just under an obelisk 2,000 feet sheer, the river plunges 900 feet, which is called the Nevada Fall. And the walls that enclose this water-magnificence are more grand than the White Mountain Notch."

Above the Nevada Fall he climbed 1500 feet again "to see the snow-streaked turrets of the great Sierras. Two of the peaks visible there, and quite near, are 13,600 feet." One of them—a noble monument to this lover of nature and eloquent eulogist of mountain scenery—is now named Mount Starr King.

PART II
ORATOR AND PATRIOT

CHAPTER I

MR. KING was so engrossed in parish duties and literary and social activities, and he was now so far removed from the centres of National thought and life, that the important political events of 1860 had passed unchallenged, if not unnoticed by him.

The lack of telegraphic communication prevented the closer acquaintance of California with the struggle that was raging in the East. "Is Lincoln elected?" Mr. King asks in a letter to a friend, dated November 7, 1860. "We are so far out of the way that we cannot find out." But he adds: "Our State has done well. Lincoln leads, as far as heard from."

Again in January 31, 1861, he writes: "California is but slightly affected as yet by the political panic. We shall adhere to the Northern Confederacy. May wisdom and grace avert bloodshed and save us from disgraceful concessions, and restore good sense and manliness to the frightened and demented South!"

But finally the reverberations of the approaching storm were heard more and more loudly in California, and the war clouds of 1861 drifted slowly over to the Pacific Coast. It was a time of great anxiety

[153]

for the loyal element in its population. Although numerically superior the Union men in California were at a disadvantage because the Federal and State officers, the military commands, the newspapers and social influences were in the hands of open or covert sympathizers with the Secession movement.

At the outbreak of the Civil War 40 per cent of the people of California were of Southern birth, while many of the Northern born were politically of their way of thinking. For ten years past this element had been in control of the State as well as of the National government. Of 53 newspapers published in California only 7 advocated the election of Abraham Lincoln, and he received only 28 per cent of its electoral vote. The Governor, Legislature and Courts, the United States Senators and Congressmen from California, were all safely Democratic and Southern in their sentiments. General Albert Sidney Johnston, a well known sympathizer with the Rebellion, and subsequently a brilliant Confederate soldier, was in command of the Federal forces in San Francisco.[1]

The danger to be apprehended was the uprising of this Southern element which was known to be well organized, armed and desperate. A secret military order, the Knights of the Golden Circle, had enrolled some 16,000 sympathizers with Secession. Joined, as they would have been, by the discontented and lawless, civil war would have ensued and an attempt

[1] "Starr King in California," by William Day Simonds. Part II.

[154]

been made to carry California out of the Union. Still others dreamed of, or openly advocated, an independent Pacific Republic, which, if consummated, would have been equally disastrous to the National idea.

There was imminent need to arouse the loyal elements in the population of California to a sense of their danger; to acquaint them with the folly and wickedness of these designs against their internal peace and the paramount authority of the National Government; to proclaim in intelligible terms the fundamental principles of the Republic, and to recall the great events in its history which confirmed them. The Union men needed a leader, the Union cause a champion to plead for it, to strengthen the timorous and vacillating, denounce treason and impart confidence in the administration at Washington. In a community in which "the love of oratory amounted to a passion," an eloquent voice was needed to inspire the people of the State, its farmers, traders, miners and stock-raisers, with the consciousness of patriotic duty, and thus prepare the way for an organization of the Union sentiment. Their brave and able leader, David C. Broderick, who a few years before had inaugurated the struggle against Southern arrogance and its aggressive endeavors in behalf of the extension of slavery, had fallen a lamented victim to it. Still another fearless and eloquent spokesman for the Union, Col. E. D. Baker, had removed to Oregon, had been elected United States Senator, and

[155]

enlisting in the Union Army soon after met a hero's death in the engagement at Ball's Bluff.

The one man on the Pacific Coast whose oratorical talents, exalted character, early training and assured political principles fitted him for this eminent service was Thomas Starr King. It found him ready and prepared for the task. Brought up under the very shadow of Bunker Hill he was unusually informed in the history of his country and the principles which underlie it. As early as 1847, by invitation of the city authorities in Charlestown, he had delivered an address on the anniversary of that early struggle of the American Revolution, in which he acutely analyzed its motive and aim,—civil, personal and religious freedom, limited only by the law of right. Again in 1852 he was the orator at the Fourth of July celebration of the municipality of Boston, choosing for his topic, "The Organization of Liberty on this Continent."

It was in February, 1861, though he was as yet unconscious of the great mission to which he was being called, that Starr King fired the opening gun of his oratorical campaign by giving at a patriotic rally in San Francisco an address on "Washington and the Union." In the month following Starr King delivered one of the most powerful and popular of his addresses, "Webster and the Constitution." A few weeks later he spoke to another great audience on "Lexington and the New Struggle for Liberty." Later themes of his patriotic appeal were "The Great

Uprising" and "The New Nation to Issue from the War." These addresses, repeated all over the State, created a great sensation and were listened to by large and delighted audiences.

"I have been lecturing on 'The New Nation to Issue from the War,'" writes Mr. King. "I gave it on June 17th before a military company here and shall have to repeat it, though the house was filled. The country districts clamor for it."

It may be permitted the present writer to say that this address was prepared at his solicitation, and during its impressive delivery the military company, the "Sumner Light Guard," of which he was a member, sat on the platform in a half-circle around the speaker, clad in the Confederate grey, which the State authorities—Southern sympathizers—had forced the California militia to wear, but which was to be exchanged, by means of the proceeds of this lecture, for uniforms of true Union blue.

Writing to a friend at the East, Rev. Thomas B. Fox, in the summer of 1861, Starr King informs him:

"We are boiling over with all sorts of agitation here. The Secessionists have taken great heart since Manassas Junction. There are three tickets for Governor and Congressman in the field, Secession-Democratic, Union-Democratic, and True-Blue Republican. The Secessionists are all of a sudden peace men, and flood the State with documents on the cost of the war, its horrors, and the propriety of stopping the fight and recognizing Jeff Davis. Ow-

[157]

ing to the division of the Union strength there begin to be fears that the Secessionists may get a plurality, and so we are arming, drilling and spouting. Among other forces to save the State I have taken to lecturing again—an hour and a half on 'The Confederate States, Old and New.' Last night, I spoke on 'Peace, and What It Would Cost Us,' for the benefit of the New York and Massachusetts Volunteers. House packed. Enthusiasm tremendous. Profits for the fund $1500. Speech printed before daylight this morning, and now flying over the State by thousands. I am to give another lecture for the same fund in two weeks."

Other letters from this period give interesting disclosures of the manifoldness of Mr. King's activities in behalf of the Union cause.

"SAN FRANCISCO, August 30th, 1860.
"We had a meeting in our church of New York men for the relief of their destitute in that State, and subscribed $2200 on the spot. We mean to raise thousands in the city and State. If we beat the Secessionists next Wednesday, Sept. 4th, at the polls, so that in spite of our Union split they can't get a plurality, we are safe. If they win, we must arm and prepare to drive the rebel Governor where Claiborn Jackson went. Perhaps you will get news of the election as soon as you get this note."

To *Randolph Ryer:*

"February 20th, 1861.
"I am in the agony of writing my long oration on Washington for the 22nd. . . . Quite an incident has

occurred here in an orthodox prayer meeting. A man got up and announced that he was called by the Almighty to rid the city of that enemy of Christ, Thomas Starr King, and that he intended to slay him as soon as a good opportunity offered, etc., etc. The prayer meeting broke up; but nothing was done to arrest the man. The chairman of our church committee the next day made an affidavit against him, he was arrested and examined, seemed quite gentle and utterly harmless on all other questions, but persisted that he was called of the Lord to plunge a dagger in my heart, and that he would, if he were to be hanged or burned the next minute.

"So he was sent to the Insane Asylum in Stockton, and 'I still live.' Poor fellow! I don't believe he would have lifted a finger upon me, because he talked so violently. If he had been really dangerous, he would have done something before talking.

To *Randolph Ryer:*

"February 24, 1861.

"I must write you a word or two of the lecture on Washington night before last. All day on the 22nd was glorious here, the city was excited on the Dis-Union question, and mass meetings were held at several points in streets and squares. It was a great and serious holiday.

"In the evening the lecture was to come off at 7:30. Tickets a dollar each. The house would comfortably seat a thousand. No tickets were given away even to the press. But there was a press there, I can tell you. Every place where a seat could be stowed was taken. They had to turn away people by the hundred who came. The dignitaries were on the stage. I laid my manuscript on a small stand

[159]

covered with the American flag. The aristocracy were on hand, lots of them from the South.

"The lecture was two hours and a quarter long— and such a time! Such stillness, and then such laughter! Such applause and then such ominous quiet when I gave them a 'free soil' touch!

"Mrs. Fremont was out and told me she hadn't been so stirred in years. . . . A son of old Vanderbilt, a Lieutenant in the Army, stayed to be introduced and tell me his joy (wasn't that a triumph!). I pitched into Secession, Concession, and Calhoun, right and left, and made Southerners applaud. I pledged California to a Northern Republic and to 'a flag that should have no treacherous threads of cotton in its warp,' and the audience came down with thunder. At the close it was announced that I would repeat it the next night, and they gave three rounds of cheers.

"But alas, yesterday I was very hoarse, and the repetition is postponed till the 4th of March! I copyrighted the address, to save it from the piracy of stenographers, and am urged to give it all over the State, and help kill the Pacific-Republic folly. It was *the* occasion, thus far, of my existence."

The *San Francisco Bulletin* reported next day: "The lucky ones who gained entrance, heard a magnificent lecture two and a quarter hours long, sparkling in every sentence, pithy, eloquent and pertinent. The delighted audience applauded to the echo."

Mr. King's younger brother, Edward, was a mariner, a man of sturdy build and modesty of nature, who used to say: "Starr has the brains of the

[160]

family, and I the brawn." Two days after Starr King's epoch-making oration on Washington, he sailed into the harbor of San Francisco in his ship, the *Syren,* and the two brothers—sky-pilot and sea-captain—met. Poetic justice should have permitted the sea-farer to be in command of the handsome clipper ship, the *Starr King,* so named by its builder and owner in Eastern Massachusetts, an admirer of our hero.

We continue our excerpts from Mr. King's letters at this crucial moment of his public career, reminding the reader that they were written in confidence to a friend, and not intended for publication.

"SAN FRANCISCO, March 10th, 1861.

"I have given my 'Washington and the Union' lecture the second time in this city. House jammed and hundreds turned away. I am to give it still again for the Masonic Relief Fund. A week from to-night I am to lecture on 'Webster and the Constitution' before our Mercantile Library Association. I shall write the lecture this week.

"I have also given the Washington lecture in Marysville and Stockton, the headquarters of 'the Chivalry,' to very large audiences. In Stockton a dozen or less Southerners hissed. I gave them cracks in return, and the house cheered and applauded like a thunder-cloud. It was a great time. The Stockton people had blistered hands next day."

"SAN FRANCISCO, March 20th, 1861.

"Last night I lectured two hours on 'Webster and the Constitution.' House filled with 1500 people at

[161]

a dollar a ticket. And they want it repeated. I didn't dwell on his 7th of March speech and the compromise of 1850. We are getting California safe out of the Southern hands.

"I am to give 'Washington' still a third time in this city, before the Masons, and also an oration April 19th before the military of the city on the 'Battle of Lexington.' "

In October, 1861, he writes an Eastern friend:

"This Sunday afternoon I preached to a regiment of Cavalry here. It was a grand sight—a thousand men in a solid square, under a cheerful California sky, listening to talk on the country, religion, etc. We have the telegraph now. I sent you a message as soon as it opened its batteries, which I hope was received. The women of our parish have equipped 2750 soldiers with towels, handkerchiefs, stockings in part, and kits containing comb, needles, thread, thimble, etc. The way the sewing machines ran and raced in our church for a month!

"I have preached to soldiers in camp and am now engaged in furnishing literature for them. But as to lecturing and organizing for the Union, there is a lull. In order to keep my hand in, I preached last Sunday twice on the telegraph. The first click of the telegraph brought in the news of Gen. Baker's death. He was a great favorite in California and the tidings dashed our joy materially."

"November 1st, 1861.

"Our hundred men for the Boston Cavalry Battalion go by this steamer. They are splendid, *perfect* fellows. I hope you will see them and speak with the Captain, who is a friend of mine. I have lectured, preached, prayed and talked for this company. They are my pets. . . . I am nearly used up in strength, though."

In the latter part of 1861, a group of American residents of Victoria, B. C., sent Mr. King a draft for one thousand dollars "in aid of the cause of American Union," together with a vigorous resolution supporting the cause of the Federal Government. It was a significant act since at that very moment there were ominous threatenings that the British Government would espouse the cause of the seceding states, in which case a war with Great Britain would have been inevitable. Starr King made effective use of this incident at a public meeting held on Sunday evening, November 24th, in San Francisco to encourage subscriptions to the National Loan. Addressing an audience of three thousand, he read to them the letter of the loyal American colony in Victoria, and by his eloquent comments upon it awoke his hearers to enthusiastic applause and practical demonstration of their equal patriotism. In his reply to the donors Mr. King wrote:

"Let us hope that this contribution from Victoria is an auspicious omen that there is to be no disruption of our peaceful bonds with England, and that no embarrassing obstacle to the triumph of law, liberty and Saxon civilization throughout our Republic is to be cast in our way by the Cabinet of Queen Victoria, which holds now the great trusts of British power and honor. A rebellion, for the sake of supporting slavery and of making the world tributary to its in-

[163]

terest, is not a cause to which the sympathies of England naturally belong. The Stars and Stripes represent the principles and hopes which make English history illustrious; and the American Government is to-day defending against traitors the seed-truths and the sacred customs which America received as an inheritance from English liberty, established, let us remember, through years of Civil War. No calamity could be greater now to the cause of civilization and freedom than a war with Great Britain, and her open aid of the rebel cause of the South. Let us aid, so far as we can, the cultivation of a good understanding and of a generous fellowship. Let us labor and pray that a spectacle so unnatural and an alliance so unholy as that just alluded to may not be seen in the high noon of this Christian century."

This letter of Starr King, widely printed and read in the journals not only of the Pacific Slope but of the East, aided in the peaceful solution of the difficulties between the two nations.

The gift of the Victoria Americans was turned over to the United States Sanitary Commission.

Writing under date of October 14, 1862, Starr King tells the readers of the *Boston Evening Transcript* the cheering story of the United States Sanitary Commission in California, of which, as its president Dr. Bellows said, he was the eloquent voice, the quickening soul. In this connection he sends for publication a poem, "Our Privilege," written in support of the Fund by "a friend, Mr. Frank Bret

Harte" (the *Transcript* spells it Haste) "who will yet be known more widely in our literature." At a previous mass meeting in San Francisco Mr. King had introduced Mr. Harte, who read a patriotic poem, "The Reveille." It was largely through Mr. King's influence that the nascent poet and romancer obtained the position as secretary of the Superintendent of the United States Mint in San Francisco which gave him the assured income and comparative leisure essential to the development of his literary talents.

In April, 1862, Mr. King writes happily to his friend Ryer: " 'Unto us a child is born, unto us a son is given.' The little emigrant stepped on the shores of time at 5 A. M. April 4th. He didn't bring much with him but a capital head and a handsome face—like his mother. But he has my nose. What shall we call the boy? Can you suggest a name? Don't say Thomas Starr, Jr. That can't be. No sir! I told the boy so plainly the first day of his existence. We had a fair understanding. He begged, and pleaded, and urged and implored, but it was of no use. He even shook his fist at me, as if demanding that it should be T. Starr the less. But I put my foot down. He sobbed and kicked but finally subsided into acquiescence." His friend Randolph Ryer had named his first-born son Starr, in memory of their friendship. Starr announces, in retaliation: "Next Sunday the baby will be baptized in church. The name is to be Frederick Randolph. The Fred-

[165]

erick is for Dr. Hedge. The Randolph is for you. Really you would be proud of your namesake if you could see him."

To *Randolph Ryer:*

"SAN FRANCISCO, January 10, 1862.

"We are all pretty well. My wife is able to walk again, and is only homesick. [Mrs. King had been struck on the knee by a loose plank in the decrepit board sidewalks of the city, and for a year suffered much pain and disability.] Edith is bright as a nest of larks. She is studying French, Latin, and Music, and is sound on the red, white and blue. She carries the national colors in her face and eyes. My wife has had a superb Christmas present, a diamond cross, from members of the parish. I do not read of any instance in the New Testament of an apostle's wife receiving a more beautiful one.

"I am hard at work as usual but not in lecturing. There is a great flood in the interior. California is a lake. Rats, squirrels, locusts, lecturers and other pests are drowned out. I am a home-bird, and enjoy it hugely. Eight discourses I have written on the Book of Job, and a lecture of an hour and a quarter on the Pilgrims for December 22nd. In fact I never wrote so much in any former years as this last year, and yet I am very strong. I grow old in looks, and am getting gray, but am feeling well. As to going back, I don't know when it will be, but not for a year from next April at any rate. I want to go East, but ought not to. There is some talk of making me Senator from California—but I would swim to Australia before taking a political post.

[166]

"The winter is very warm, once we saw ice in the city, just a skim of it, but roses bloom in the open air. The parish is strong, out of debt and interested in good works. We have the telegraph now, and hear of the fluctuations and wretched conduct of the war."

To the same.

"SAN FRANCISCO, January 20th, 1862.

"I send you a copy of my address at the grave of Colonel Baker. I attended a private funeral service at his wife's and daughter's residence before the public ceremony. I knew the Colonel and found him a very able and brilliant man. His daughter is a parishioner of mine. He is a great loss to this coast."

A lecture by Mr. King on "The Privilege and Duties of Patriotism" sets forth, as does no other of his public addresses, the central thought and purpose of these activities in behalf of the undivided Union of States. By permission of the publishers of Starr King's writings passages from this oration are given below. Yet as we transcribe them we feel how inadequately the written or printed page reproduces the spoken word of the orator, or preserves the impression it made on his auditors. As Mr. King himself tells us:

"Alas for the perishableness of eloquence! It is the only thing in the higher walks of human creativeness that passes away. The statue lives after the sculptor dies, as sublime as when his chisel left it. St. Peter's is a perpetual memorial and utterance of

[167]

the great mind of Angelo. The Iliad is as fresh to-day as twenty-five centuries ago. The picture may grow richer with years. But great oratory, the most delightful and marvellous of the expressions of moral power, passes and dies with the occasion."

Yet if the strains of the great singers who captivate the hearts of men to-day; if the sweet music of violin and flute and harp may be recorded and reproduced at will to the delight of later generations, may we not hope that by the perfecting of mechanical inventions the voice and inflections of future orators and preachers may be preserved for the edification of posterity?

Said Starr King:

"I am to speak to you of the Privilege and Duties of American Patriotism.

"First the Privilege. Patriotism is love of country. It is a privilege that we are capable of such a sentiment. Self-love is the freezing-point in the temperature of the world. As the heart is kindled and ennobled it pours out feeling and interest, first upon family and kindred, then upon country, then upon humanity. The home, the flag, the cross,—these are the representatives or symbols of the noblest and most sacred affections or treasures of feeling in human nature.

"We sometimes read arguments by very strict moralists which cast a little suspicion upon the value of patriotism as a virtue, for the reason that the law of love, unrestricted love, should be our guide and inspiration. We must be cosmopolitan by our sym-

pathy, they prefer to say. Patriotism, if it inter-
feres with the wider spirit of humanity, is sectional-
ism of the heart. We must not give up to country
'what is meant for mankind.'

"Such sentiments may be uttered in the interest of
Christian philanthropy, but they are not healthy.
The Divine method in evoking our noblest affections is always from particulars to generals. God
'hath set the solitary in families,' and bound the families into communities, and organized communities
into nations; and he has ordained special duties for
each of these relationships, and inspired affections
to prompt the discharge of them, and to exalt the
character.

"The law of love is the principle of the spiritual
universe just as gravitation is the governing force of
space. It binds each particle of matter to every
other particle, but it attracts inversely as the square
of the distance, and thus becomes practically a series
of local or special forces, holding our feet perpetually to one globe, and allowing only a general unity,
which the mind appropriates through science and
meditation, with the kindred but far-off spheres.
The man that has most of the sentiment of love will
have the most intense special affections. You cannot love the whole world and nobody in particular.
If you try that, it will be true of you as of the miser
who said, 'what I give is nothing to nobody.' However deep his baptism in general good-will, a man
must look with a thrill that nothing else can awaken,
into the face of the mother that bore him; he cannot
cast off the ties that bind him to filial responsibilities
and a brother's devotion; and Providence has ordained that out of identity of race, a common history, the same scenery, literature, laws, and aims,—

[169]

though in perfect harmony with good-will to all men, —the wider family feeling, the distinctive virtue, patriotism, should spring. If the ancient Roman could believe that the yellow Tiber was the river dearest to Heaven; if the Englishman can see a grandeur in the Thames which its size will not suggest; if the Alpine storm-wind is a welcome home-song to the Swiss mountaineer; if the Laplander believes that his country is the best the sun shines upon; if the sight of one's own national flag in other lands will at once awaken feelings that speed the blood and melt the eyes; if the poorest man will sometimes cherish a proud consciousness of property in the great deeds that glow upon his country's annals and in the monuments of its power,—let us confess that the heart of man, made for the Christian law, was made also to contract a special friendship for its native soil, its kindred stock, its ancestral traditions,—let us not fail to see that where the sentiment of patriotism is not deep, a sacred affection is absent, an essential element of virtue is wanting, and religion is barren of one prominent witness of its sway.

"But why argue in favor of patriotism as a lofty virtue? History refuses to countenance the analytic ethics of spiritual dreamers. It pushes into notice Leonidas, Tell, Cincinnatus, Camillus, Hampden, Winkelried, Scipio, Lafayette, Adams, Bolivar, and Washington, in whom the sentiment has become flesh, and gathered to itself the world's affections and honors. It asks us, 'What do you say of these men? These are among the brighter jewels of my kingdom. Thousands of millions fade away into the night in my realm, but these souls shine as stars, with purer lustre as they retreat into the blue of time. Is not their line of greatness as legitimate as that of poets, philosophers, philanthropists, and priests?' . . .

NATIONAL PATRIOTISM

"It is a privilege of our nature, hardly to be measured, that we are capable of the emotion of patriotism, that we can feel a nation's life in our veins, rejoice in a nation's glory, suffer for a nation's momentary shame, throb with a nation's hope. . . .

"Think of a man living in one of the illustrious civilized communities of the world, and insensible to its history, honor, and future,—say of England! Think of an intelligent inhabitant of England so wrapped in selfishness that he has no consciousness of the mighty roots of that kingdom, nor of the toughness of its trunk, nor of the spread of its gnarled boughs! Runnymede and Agincourt are behind him, but he is insensible to the civil triumph and the knightly valor. All the literature that is crowned by Bacon, Shakespeare, and Milton, the noblest this earth ever produced from one national stock, awakens in him no heart-beat of pride. He reads of the sturdy blows in the great rebellion, and of the gain to freedom by the later and more quiet revolution, and it is no more to him than if the record had been dropped from another planet. The triumphs of English science over nature, the hiss of her engines, the whirl of her wheels, the roar of her factory drums, the crackle of her furnaces, the beat of her hammers, the vast and chronic toil that mines her treasures, affect him with no wonder and arouse no exultant thrill of partnership. And he sees nothing and feels nothing that stirs his torpid blood in the strokes and sweep of that energy, before which

[171]

the glory of Waterloo and Trafalgar is dim, which
has knit to the English will colonies and empires
within a century which number nearly one fourth of
the inhabitants of the globe. The red flag of England hung out on all her masts, from all her house-
tops, and from every acre of her conquests and possessions, would almost give this planet the color of
Mars, if seen through a telescope from a neighbor-
ing star. What a privilege to be a conscious fibre of
that compacted force! If I were an Englishman,
I should be proud every hour of every day over my
heritage. . . . The man who is dead to such pride
ought not to be rated as a man.

"And is it any less a privilege to be an American?
Suppose that the continent could turn towards you
to-morrow at sunrise, and show to you the whole
American area in the short hours of the sun's advance from Eastport to the Pacific! You would see
New England roll into light from the green plumes
of Aroostook to the silver stripe of the Hudson; west-
ward thence over the Empire State, and over the
lakes, and over the sweet valleys of Pennsylvania,
and over the prairies, the morning blush would run
and would waken all the line of the Mississippi;
from the frosts where it rises, to the fervid waters in
which it pours; for three thousand miles it would
be visible, fed by rivers that flow from every mile
of the Alleghany slope, and edged by the green em-
broideries of the temperate and tropic zones; beyond
this line another basin, too, the Missouri, catching
the morning, leads your eye along its western slope,
till the Rocky Mountains burst upon the vision, and
yet do not bar it; across its passes we must follow,
as the stubborn courage of American pioneers has
forced its way, till again the Sierra and their silver

veins are tinted along the mighty bulwark with the break of day; and then over to the gold-fields of the western slope, and the fatness of the California soil, and the beautiful valleys of Oregon, and the stately forests of Washington, the eye is drawn, as the globe turns out of the night-shadow, and when the Pacific waves are crested with radiance, you have the one blending picture, nay, the reality, of the American domain! No such soil, so varied by climate, by products, by mineral riches, by forest and lake, by wild heights and buttresses, and by opulent plains,—yet all bound into unity of configuration and bordered by both warm and icy seas,—no such domain was ever given to one people.

THE LESSON OF HISTORY

"And then suppose that you could see in a picture as vast and vivid the preparation for our inheritance of this land:—Columbus haunted by his round idea and setting sail in a sloop to see Europe sink behind him, while he was serene in the faith of his dream; the later navigators of every prominent Christian race who explored the upper coasts; the Mayflower with her cargo of sifted acorns from the hardy stock of British puritanism, and the ship, whose name we know not, that bore to Virginia the ancestors of Washington; the clearing of the wilderness, and the dotting of its clearings with the proofs of manly wisdom and Christian trust; then the gradual interblending of effort and interest and sympathy into one life, the congress of the whole Atlantic slope to resist oppression upon one member, the rally of every State around Washington and his holy sword, and again the nobler rally around him when he signed the Constitution, and after that the organization of

[173]

the farthest West with North and South into one polity and communion; when this was finished, the tremendous energy of free life, under the stimulus and with the aid of advancing science, in increasing wealth, subduing the wilds to the bonds of use, multiplying fertile fields, and busy schools, and noble workshops, and churches hallowed by free-will offerings of prayer, and happy homes, and domes dedicated to the laws of states that rise by magic from the haunts of the buffalo and deer, all in less than a long lifetime; and if we could see also how, in achieving this, the flag which represents all this history is dyed in traditions of exploits, by land and sea, that have given heroes to American annals whose names are potent to conjure with, while the world's list of thinkers in matter is crowded with the names of American inventors, and the higher rolls of literary merit are not empty of the title of our 'representative men':—if all that the past has done for us and the present reveals could thus stand apparent in one picture, and then if the promise of the future to the children of our millions under our common law, and with continental peace, could be caught in one vast spectral exhibition, the wealth in store, the power, the privilege, the freedom, the learning, the expansive and varied and mighty unity in fellowship, almost fulfilling the poet's dream of

'The Parliament of man, the federation of the world,'

you would exclaim with exultation, 'I, too, am an American!' You would feel that patriotism, next to your tie to the Divine Love, is the greatest privilege of your life; and you would devote yourselves, out of inspiration and joy, to the obligations of patriotism, that this land, so spread, so adorned, so colonized, so blessed, should be kept forever one in polity, in spirit, and in aims! . . .

"True patriotism is pledged to the idea which one's native country represents. It does not accept and glory in its country merely for what it is at present and has been in the past, but for what it may be. Each nation has a representative value. Each race that has appropriated a certain latitude which harmonizes with its blood has the capacity to work out special good results, and to reveal great truths in some original forms. God designs that each country shall bear a peculiar ideal physiognomy, and he has set its geographical characteristics as a bony skeleton, and breathed into it a free life spirit, which, if loyal to the intention, will keep the blood in health, infuse vigor into every limb, give symmetry to the form, and carry the flush of a pure and distinct expression to the countenance. It is the patriot's office to study the laws of public growth and energy, and to strive with enthusiastic love to guard against every disease that would cripple the frame, that he may prevent the lineaments of vice and brutality from degrading the face which God would have radiant with truth, genius, and purity.

"He was the best patriot of ancient Greece who had the widest and wisest conception of the capacities and genius of Greece, and labored to paint that ideal winningly before the national mind, and to direct the flame of national aspiration, fanned by heroic memories, up to the noblest possibilities of Grecian endeavor. The truest patriot of England would be the man whose mind should see in the English genius and geography what that nation could do naturally and best for humanity, and, seizing the traditional

[175]

elements that are in harmony with that possibility, should use them to enliven his own sympathies, and to quicken the nation's energy. We might say the same of Russia and Italy. The forward look is essential to patriotism.

"And how much more emphatically and impressively true is this when we bring our own country into the foreground! We have been placed on our domain for the sake of a hope. What we have done, and what has been done for us, is only preparation, the outline-sketching of a picture to be filled with color and life in the next three centuries. Shall the sketch be blurred and the canvas be torn in two? That is what we are to decide in these bitter and bloody days.

NATIONAL UNITY

"Our struggle now is to keep the country from falling away from the idea which every great patriot has recognized as the purpose towards which our history, from the first, has been moving. God devised the scheme for us of one republic. He planted the further slope of the Alleghanies at first with Saxon men; he has striped the Pacific Coast with the energy of their descendants, protecting thus both avenues of entrance to our domain against European intrusion; but the great wave of population he has rolled across the Alleghanies into the central basin. That is the seat of the American polity. And an imperial river runs through it to embarrass, and to shame, and to balk all plans of rupture. The Mississippi bed was laid by the Almighty as the keel of the American ship, and the channel of every stream that pours into it is one of its ribs. We have just covered the mighty frame with planking, and have

[176]

divided the hull into State compartments. And the rebels say, 'Break the ship in two.' They scream, 'We have a right to, on the ground of the sovereignty of the compartments, and the principles of the Declaration of Independence; we have a right to, and we will!' The loyal heart of the nation answers, 'We will knock out all your Gulf compartments and shiver your sovereign bulkheads, built of ebony, to pieces, and leave you one empty territory again, before you shall break the keel.' That is the right answer. We must do it, not only for our own safety, but to preserve the idea which the nation has been called to fulfil, and to which patriotism is called and bound to be loyal. Aye, even if there were one paragraph or line in the Declaration of Independence that breathed or hinted a sanction of the rebellion! Geology is older than the pen of Jefferson; the continent is broader than the Continental Congress; and they must go to the foundations to learn their statesmanship.

"The Procrustes bed of American patriotism is the bed of the Mississippi, and every theory of national life and every plan for the future must be stretched on that; and woe to its wretched bones and sockets if it naturally reaches but half-way!

"Providence made the country, too, when the immense basin should be filled with its fitting millions, to show the world the beauty and economy of continental peace. It is a destiny radically different from that of Europe, with its four millions of armed men, that has been indicated for us. By the interplay of widely different products into one prosperity —cotton and cattle, tobacco and corn, metals and manufactures, shipyards and banking rooms, forests and fields,—and all under one law, and all enjoying

[177]

local liberty,—sufficient centralization, but the mildest pressure on the subordinate districts and the personal will—Providence designed to bless us with immense prosperity, to develop an energy unseen before on this globe, and to teach the nations a lesson which would draw them into universal fraternity and peace.

"The rebels have tried to frustrate this hope and scheme. Patriotism, which discerns the idea to which the nation is thus called, arms to prevent its defeat. They say that there shall not be such unified prosperity and all-embracing peace for the future hundreds of millions on our domain. We say that there shall. And we arm to enforce our vision.

"But is not that a strange way to establish peace, by fighting on such a scale as the republic now witnesses? Is it not a novel method to labor for economy of administration and expense in government by a war which will fetter the nation with such a debt? We answer, the rebellion gave the challenge, and now victory at any cost is the only economy. Carnage, if they will it, is the only path to peace.

'For our own good
All causes shall give way; we are in blood
Stept in so far, that, should we wade no more,
Returning were as tedious as go o'er.'

Yes, if we return, all our blood and treasures are wasted. The peace we gain by victory is for all the future, and for uncounted millions. The debt we incur by three years' fighting will be nothing compared with the new energy and security aroused, nothing to the next hundred years. And it will establish the idea to which the land was dedicated."

[178]

CHAPTER II

AS the nation plunged deeper and deeper into war, it became evident that Starr King had not underestimated the arduousness of the campaign in which he was enlisted, and the drain on his own powers which it involved. "What a time to live in," he wrote to a friend, "worth all other times ever known in our history or any other." Only one thought now possessed him, his duty to his country. His health, always delicate, had been severely tried by the exacting nature of his California experiances. We find him writing to the chairman of his parish: "It is useless to disguise the fact that I am not as well as I was when in Boston. I experience strange debility and singular pains and numbness in the brain. For writing purposes I am nearly worthless." But, he said to a friend, "I had rather die next year than be sick this." Arousing himself he journeyed again and again over the State, the eloquent champion of union and liberty. Everywhere he met with enthusiastic welcome, and his popularity and influence became unbounded. His course in preparing the public mind for the deeper issues of the war displayed rare judgment and tact. At first his

[179]

utterances were all for the maintenance of the Union.
With unanswerable logic he proved the necessity for
its preservation, and exposed the fallacy and unjusti-
fiableness of the Rebellion against the Central Government. "Rebellion," he declared, "sins against
the Mississippi, it sins against the coast line, it sins
against the ballot box, it sins against oaths of allegiance, it sins against public and beneficent progress
and history and hope—the worth of the laborer, the
rights of man. It strikes for barbarism against civilization."

Growing bolder and more confident he would feel
his audiences with an occasional reference to the question of negro soldiery, striving to uproot the prejudices they might entertain against this war measure.
"Cannon balls are black," he would say, "war does
not whitewash them. Powder is black. War does
not bleach it. Why then, this absurd prejudice
against a race of the same color *in the grain* as you
and I?" Soon the responses came thicker and faster.
The popular mind grew with the public necessity.
He could give utterance to the most radical sentiments and meet only applause, and bursting its
shackles of diplomacy his eloquence thrilled them
with its fervent appeals for the equal rights of all
men, white or black.

Referring to the ardently awaited Proclamation
emancipating the Slaves, he declared with passionate
eagerness: "O that the President would soon speak
that electric sentence,—inspiration to the loyal North,

[180]

doom to the traitorous aristocracy whose cup of guilt is full. Let him say that it is a war of mass against class, of America against feudalism, of the school-master against the slave-master, of workmen against the barons, of the ballot-box against the Barracoon. This is what the struggle means. Proclaim it so, and what a light breaks through our leaden sky! The ocean-wave rolls then with the impetus and weight of an idea."

These patriotic sentiments were uppermost in all his public utterances at the time. When he gave a course of lectures on the American poets it was to show that their underlying inspiration was their faith in freedom and the rights of men, their love of country and humanity; to thrill his hearers by reciting the latest patriotic verses which his literary friends, Longfellow, Holmes, Bryant, Whittier, Lowell, had sent him in advance of their publication at the East. Was "Paradise Lost" his theme? It was to find in the fallen angels and their doom a parallel with the seceding states of the South.

This literary activity for the Union cause will explain the following letters to Eastern correspondents.

To *Dr. Henry W. Bellows:*

"SAN FRANCISCO, October, 1862.
"I have a matter to speak of, which is very delicate.
"We are to build a new church here at a cost of about fifty thousand dollars. Added to that the land cost eighteen thousand. Then a new organ,

[181]

to be built out here (one of my hobbies), to cost four thousand, and all to be paid for in a year. It will be a very hard pull. But I must carry it through, in spite of war and all other calls for money. For I ought to leave here, year after next, if the war shall cease, to get a little rest, even if I return here afterwards.

"Now I have promised to furnish the new organ, as my gift, besides subscribing to the church building. A thousand dollars already are secured. And about New Year I shall give a course of lectures here on prominent American poets—Bryant, Longfellow, Holmes, Whittier, Lowell, partly to sweeten our civilization, and partly to help along the organ fund.

"I think that Holmes, Whittier and Lowell will each send to me a short piece which has never been printed, to read at the close of the lecture devoted to them. Has Bryant anything in manuscript which could be sent to me to read at the close of the introductory lecture which will be devoted to his verse? The reading of a piece here would not hinder the publication in any shape at the East. And I am sure that the course of lectures will help civilization here, increase the demand for our best literature, and supply a golden strand for the cable that is to bind this coast to the East. I dare not ask Mr. Bryant directly: perhaps *you* will think it not unbecoming to make the suggestions, and you may feel sure that his kindness, if the request can be granted, will not be indelicately used. If he has any war-verses, or wishes to say anything further about the Oregon, that hears now so many other sounds than its own dashings, how welcome they would be! Of course, I must know very soon if I can hope for such a great favor to our city, and if anything is sent, it had better come by Wells, Fargo's Express by steamer.

"T. S. K."

It was sent—Bryant's war poem, the first verse of which reads:

"O country, marvel of the earth!
O realm to sudden greatness grown!
The age that gloried in thy birth,
Shall it behold thee overthrown?
Shall traitors lay that greatness low?
No, land of Hope and Blessing, No!"

To *William R. Alger:*

"SAN FRANCISCO, December, 1862.

"Will you take this to Jas. T. Fields—dear James —and say that I am just made happy by the despatch from Bellows in which, among other things, he lightningizes the news that poems from Longfellow, Holmes and Whittier will go Californiaward by steamer of the 11th of Dec. Thank James superbly, and ask him piteously, beseechingly, if Lowell won't also send one! It would be such a treat here, and Lowell is so popular, and could touch the heart of this State so electrically by a direct message. Tell James T. also not to forget my request to *his* poetic ink-stand. I know the ink is ready and it will run free if he will dip his pen in. I embrace James T. and expect him to feel the squeeze so that the two poems will appear!"

Mr. King's pulpit was draped throughout the whole of this eventful period with the American flag, and not infrequently the rumble of half-suppressed

[183]

applause at the sentiments of the preacher ran through the pews. The titles of some of his sermons indicated the character of their teaching. Such were "The Choice between Barrabas and Jesus"; "The Fall of Dagon before the Ark"; "The Treason of Judas Iscariot"; "The Nation's New Year"; (1863). Starr King had no fear of political preaching. "He believed the pulpit to be the prow of the Ship of State, and that its mission was to point the way in all the great moral crises of the nation."

Writing to Edward Everett Hale, he tells him:

"I arranged last week for a grand jubilee thanksgiving service in our church on Sunday morning, February 23. We have Trenkle as organist, you know. And our quartette choir is admirable. We doubled it; selected the great battle psalms for responsive chanting, the Columbiad passages of prophecy for Scripture reading, prayers and exultations from Judas Maccabeus (Handel's, not Apocrypha's), with a Gloria of Mozart for the official music, and Holmes's Army Hymn for the congregation to lift in an artillery chorus to the Lutheran passion of Old Hundred; and thus enjoyed ourselves, with a crowd that packed the house. Hundreds went away from the doors. I felt the whole fervor of the congregation pour through me, and came near going off the handle in the address which brought down the house. Since Sunday I have been disturbed in the heart region, and to-night am quite weak and a little feverish. But I have squared accounts with that pain in the head for Bull Run. So please to be more moderate with your victories, unless you mean to kill some of us out here. One a week is all we can bear."

The labor of preparing his lectures and addresses now became overpowering. He had rarely attempted extemporaneous speaking, and then with no marked success. "I have not got," he would say, "the faculty of thinking on my feet, as Beecher has it." All his great war-time addresses were carefully dictated or written out by himself, and read to his audiences from the manuscript. Only by the electric quality of his delivery and his admirable elocution was he enabled to read his written speeches with such effect. Mrs. Jessie Fremont recounts that when Senator Baker of Oregon on his way to join his regiment at the East, addressed a great meeting in Platt's Hall, Mr. King went with General and Mrs. Fremont to hear him. As he listened to Baker's splendid periods and saw their powerful effect on his audience, he walked up and down the private box they were occupying, in great excitement, saying again and again, "That is the true way to reach men! I can never do that. How I envy him!" But Mr. King was soon compelled to make the attempt, and his success in extempore speech was as much a surprise to himself as it was gratifying to his friends. In this improvised speaking the orator was even more apparent.

A characteristic of Starr King's oratorical style was the frequent length of his sentences. This peculiarity was due in part to the lightning-like rapidity

[185]

of his thought and imagination, and his astounding fecundity of language, but even more to his habit of dictating his sermons and lectures to an amanuensis, a method unfavorable to literary condensation and brevity of expression. Had Mr. King lived to revise his public utterances before they were submitted to the printer, they would doubtless have undergone some changes in literary form likely to make them more acceptable to the reader. This drawback—if such it was—was less noticeable in his public speaking; indeed it seemed to add to its effectiveness. As his sentences developed, each successive stroke gave new depth and beauty to the verbal picture, each added illustration made it more convincing, sweeping his listeners with ever-accumulating power to acceptance of its final and irresistible appeal. As when a great wave out at sea lifts itself in successive upheavals above the surrounding surface, and rushes on, billow on billow, to the distant shore, overcoming every obstacle, absorbing into itself every backward current, finally with tremendous accumulated power to reach its goal and hurl its watery mass in foaming and resounding fury upon the beach, so Starr King by the impassioned fervor of his delivery carried his hearers irresistibly on through the mazes of his argument, overcoming successively their prejudices, doubts and fears, until, as he reached the conclusion, the cumulative effect of his oratory was shown by their enthusiastic acceptance of his sentiments and their uproarious applause.

CAMPAIGN FOR THE UNION

I recall that on one occasion at a public rejoicing over Union victories in the field, the great audience in Union Hall was restless and only half-attentive until Mr. King took a seat on the platform. Then a welcoming burst of applause overpowered the voice of the Union candidate for Governor who was addressing them, and in a few moments he yielded the floor to Starr King. The latter came forward. The swaying mass of men on the floor below, packed breast to back, quieted down in an instant. With their eyes riveted on him they listened in deep silence, a silence only broken by the applause and cheering which his words elicited.

Thus he held them enthralled, fascinated, until in closing his powerful address he drew for them the word-picture of a battle-field. The rush and din of the struggle, the wave on wave of alternate advance and retreat, the clash of arms, the agony, the triumph, were all delineated with wonderful fidelity and force.

As he retired from the platform, an answering cheer went up from three thousand throats that shook the building to its foundations.

A moment later, in company with Frank Bret Harte, I sought him. We found Mr. King lying on a sofa in the anteroom, pale and exhausted. "What a triumph!" said Harte. "How did you manage to get through that long last sentence?" "I hardly know," returned Mr. King, "I seemed quite unconscious of my surroundings. My imagination beheld

the scenes, my mind worked out the sentences moments before I uttered them."

Mr. King's admirable work in behalf of the United
States Sanitary Commission for the sick and wounded
soldiers deserves unstinted praise. By his urgent advice in the committee room not to divide and squander
their fund among the many applications for it, and by
his eloquent appeals in public, California's splendid
contribution of over one million and a quarter of dollars—one fourth of the amount contributed by the
entire country—to this cause was mainly assured.

In a letter to Edward Everett Hale, he describes
the beginning of his activities in this cause:

"In my speech I tried to shame our city for its
tardiness and indifference on the wounded soldiers
question. The papers took up the note, and last
Sunday night we had a mass meeting in Platt's great
hall in this city to stir up the people to action. Four
prominent lawyers spoke, and I closed the talking
with an extempore appeal of three-quarters of an
hour. It was a glorious meeting. And this week
we have sent on by telegraph, as first instalment of
our subscriptions, one hundred thousand dollars
to the Sanitary Commission. We shall do a great
deal more next week, and I hope another hundred
thousand. Pray Heaven it may go to victorious
wounded! But alas! we have no proof as yet that
we have the brains to lead our forces. But why
speculate three weeks ahead?

"I have kept well in all the labor and distraction.
It is only this week that I feel used up."

Fitz-Hugh Ludlow, the Secretary and historian

of this National philanthropy, tells us: "Starr King *was* the Sanitary Commission in California."

Letters written to Dr. Bellows, President of the United States Sanitary Commission, the clumsily named Soldier's Relief Association of the Civil War, disclose the truth of this statement.

"SAN FRANCISCO, March 18, 1862.
"My dear Bellows:

"I received some time ago your eloquent acknowledgments of the Victoria cash. Your note was forwarded to the good British Yankees, and produced an effect even before it reached them. For while it was on the way I received another letter from the Committee in Victoria, enclosing a draft for three hundred dollars more. We always thought of you, dear Bellows, superior to all ordinary laws that hedge and hamper human action. This Victoria feat proves that you can raise an echo before your will reaches the point of resistance.

"What to do with the three hundred? Of course, we couldn't send such a trifle to the Commission. Well, we have an Olympic Club of gentlemen-athletes here who gave an exhibition not long ago for the benefit of our volunteers, at which I cut up some antics of speech in an opening address. I made them shell off two hundred dollars from their Patriotic Corn Cob. Still further, we have a small association here called 'The Ladies' Patriotic Fund Society.' Some weeks ago they gave a Festival, at the opening of which I speechified and read Mrs. Howe's 'Weave no more silk, ye Lyons looms.' The festival cleared $1500 for the benefit of our volunteers in this State. Last Saturday, I met the Committee of excellent

[189]

women, and tried my luck at milking that fund also for your benefit. It 'gave down' five hundred dollars, after I had pledged myself that the amount should be restored if occasion should come in the future for its use here. (I mean restored by a lecture or festival here, not by you, of course.) The ladies seemed very glad to serve the objects of the Commission, and voted heartily to accede to my request, although their 'Constitution' looked on aghast at the work.

"So you see I have gathered another thousand for your noble work. Our collector of the port has hopes, too, of sending you a contribution from funds placed at his discretion. I hope he will be able to make up still another thousand. If our flood-visitation had not come, we could have done more for you, but all sympathy and energy for two months were drawn towards the one sacred duty of protecting the homeless and clothing the naked who flocked by hundreds to us from their ruined farms in the interior.

"We have been greatly excited here over the 'forward march' from Washington. The telegraph first told us that there had been a great battle at Manassas and a total rout of the enemy. Afterwards we learned that it was a retreat of the latter. When the flag streams over Richmond and Charleston, things will look right, so far as battle is concerned. But the settlement and reconstruction! Have we statesmen wise and strong enough to draw the fitting plan? I see all the difficulties in the way of a summary treatment of the slave question, and yet if its Moloch-arrogance isn't crushed, Jeff Davis will be elected the next President of the Nation.

"Have you met Mrs. Fremont? I hope so. Her husband I am very little acquainted with; but she is sublime, and carries guns enough to be formidable to a whole Cabinet,—a She-Merrimac, thoroughly sheathed, and carrying fire in the genuine Benton-furnaces.

"I read all your addresses and reported speeches with great admiration. Your 'Birth-pangs of the Gospel' is a stream of moral electricity. If the war lasts a year longer, how are you to manage living? Of course you will burn out before then. I think many of us will collapse when the settlement is made, —go out with the Peace, as people often in consumption 'go out with the tide.' May it not be that we shall go out with shame at the terms of the Peace!

"But I am boring you. Take the thousand dollars with our best feeling for the Sanitary Commission, and write me again a receipt for it, to show that I am not a disciple of Cameron, or of that earlier Simon who traded in the Holy Ghost. I am worn out and yet on the tread-mill. How I ache to see you all! Give my love to the Saints—Livermore, Osgood, Frothingham, Chapin. Tell them to keep a little corner in their hearts and memories for me, and believe me, dear Bellows,

"Truly and warmly,
"Yours, T. S. KING."

To the same:

"SAN FRANCISCO, October 10, 1862.

"This will be handed to you by our excellent Congressman, Hon. A. A. Sargent, a bright, honest, able and handsome man. It is not for me to introduce him to you. He carries with him the best possible card and commendation, in the six thousand dollars of pure gold which his home city here, Nevada, has entrusted to him for the Commission, and

[191]

the twelve thousand dollar draft of which he is the bearer from Marysville. I helped stir up the Marysville saints to their good works. Nevada, having Sargent in it, needed no other stimulant. And both towns will do more for the Fund.

"In fact, the State is just waking up. We are tasting the pleasure of doing our duty, and every county here aches for some of your eloquence as a special and local bounty and dainty. I advise you to keep your eloquence-reservoir well supplied, with the faucet free, for several weeks to come.

"My wife encloses with this note a draft for the fund of $536.80, which she has bought with some money sent to her to-day from some ladies in Santa Clara, a village about forty miles from our city. Julia is Treasurer of our Ladies' Lint Association here, of which Mrs. Swain is Secretary, and Mrs. Winchester, who goes to New York by this steamer, President. They send some lint, etc., to you by this vessel, and will send more on the 21st.

"You have received our second hundred thousand with the request to send thirty of it to St. Louis. Our Committee were grievously afflicted in being obliged to stipulate with you at all as to distribution. They are so delighted with your dispatches and so thoroughly reliant upon your judgment, that they wanted to pour the money into your hands and give you carte blanche. To prevent any controversy between St. Louis and New York, our Committee, much to their regret, were obliged to ask you to send from the second hundred thousand enough to make fifty thousand. You will not be hampered hereafter by our Committee, who are unanimously in favor of making you Commander in Chief now, and successor to Uncle Abe in 1864!

[192]

CAMPAIGN FOR THE UNION

"The State continues to do nobly in contributions. They are not complete yet in any counties, and therefore we have received but little in the city of what has been subscribed. But I think that a hundred thousand dollars has been pledged already outside of San Francisco, which will soon find its way into your sacred purse. I want the State to come up to half a million. To-morrow I am to speak at a mass meeting in one of our farming counties. Last night I addressed an Agricultural Fair, and closed with an appeal for the Fund. Next week and week after I shall be in the same business. And all this while the rebel congress are discussing the project of an address to the Pacific Coast in behalf of an alliance offensive and defensive! It could be nothing but *offensive.*

"When shall we strike again from the Potomac? 'Little Mac' still hugs the Maryland shore. Pope was a flatulent soul; but if McClellan turns out a genius, there is no truth in physiognomy. He would do to invest Gibraltar, or bombard Teneriffe, or attack any fossil concern that couldn't change outline, but a foe that has alertness and two ideas an hour beats him after he has won a victory. And Halleck is fit for one bureau in the War Department. He is a man of the reddest tape. Bellows, make a dash for the chief command! You could do the thing and save us!

"Yours,
"T. S. KING."

To the same:

"SAN FRANCISCO, Oct. 20, 1862.
"Behold duplicate of draft, of which original went to you by Congressman Sargent on the 11th inst. I

[193]

THOMAS STARR KING

don't know that you look at such small amounts as
five hundreds in these days of the California hydraulic streams. Lots of little towns here are eager to
put their knuckles to your battery, and get a spark
and shock. I am trying to stop them and save you,
and I hope to succeed. I am laboring to get the
State contributions massed in San Francisco, and
hurled at you by tens of thousands. We send on
thirty thousand to-morrow. Are we not doing well?

"Your letter to our Committee, in reply to the first
remittance of a hundred thousand, takes everybody
down here. It is a glorious gush of eloquence, and
touches California exactly in the right spot. The
only mistake was in your allusion to the individuals
that have helped the fund, etc. Who can they be?
I shall speak this week in the interior to stir up the
fund-contributions. San Francisco is to-day *the
most loyal city* of the nation.

"T. S. KING."

To the same.

"SAN FRANCISCO, October 28th, 1862.

"You must be tired, by this time, of seeing my
signature and the postmark of San Francisco. Bear
up a little longer and we will slacken. Contributions still pour in for the fund. Last week I spoke
four nights in the interior, as a sort of rowelling
process on the conscience, and every time with promise of good results.

"Last week, also, we published a circular which
I enclose, that you may see how you and I are put
into the same sheets in California. I am only an
Honorary Member of the Relief Committee here;
but I draw up their circulars and advise them as to

[194]

movements, etc. Otis, Norris, Redington and Mc-Ruer are members of our parish. Lent would be if he did not live forty miles away. I drew up the enclosed circular, which has been sent all over our hundred square miles, to supply the final stimulant to the out-of-the-way regions where speakers cannot go. I think it will ensure fifty thousand dollars additional contribution, which will yield good California interest on the cost of printing.

"T. S. KING."

From all sides now came calls for his services. "To-night," he writes humorously from the mining town of Yreka, "I am to speak in a village with the sweet name of Dead Wood, and to-morrow at the very important and cultivated settlement of Rough and Ready. Scott's Bar wants me; Horsetown is after me; Mugginsville bids high; Oro Fino applies with a long petition of names. Mad Mule has not yet sent in a request; nor Piety Hill, nor Modesty Gulch; but doubtless they will be heard from in due time. The Union sentiment is strong; but the secessionists are watchful and not in despair."

He was as effective with rough miners and cowboys as with cultivated city audiences. Mr. King declared that he never knew the exhilaration of public speaking until he faced a front row of revolvers and bowie knives. "On one occasion," we are told, "when every seat in the building where he spoke was occupied, the aisles and entry packed, and a compact mass of people on the sidewalk, a tall, rough miner on the extreme edge of the crowd, who was listening in an

[195]

ecstasy of delight, nudged his shorter companion
and exclaimed: 'I say, Jim, stand on your toes and
get a sight of him! Why, the boy is taking every
trick!'" On another occasion, his impassioned plea
for union and liberty was interrupted by a solitary
hiss. Pausing for a moment Starr King remarked,
"There are only two kinds of animals that express
themselves by a hiss—the goose and the snake."
Then, pointing to the offender he cried: "Behold
the Copperhead!" He responded to every invitation; his labors were endless and untiring. "I
should be broken down," he wrote a friend, "if I
had time to think of how I feel, but I haven't."

On his Columbia River trip occurred an incident
of which he made effective use in his public addresses.
On the deck of the steamer he heard a man declaim-
ing to his fellow-passengers in behalf of secession
and slavery. For an instant, he said, he was possessed
by a wild impulse to seize the traitor by the throat
and hurl him into the stream below. But he re-
frained, for he remembered that its waters were
clean!

This incident brings to mind a charge brought
against Mr. King that in his oratorical fervor he in-
dulged sometimes in outbursts of invective and denunciation against the personal character and motives
of the enemies of his country and his kind. But let
it be remembered that as the champion of the national
idea he was confronted not only by reactionary traditions and the immobility of established institutions

and vested interests. He found himself opposed also by personal antagonists, well-organized, rancorous, and unscrupulous, actively at work in defaming him and defeating his purposes. It was inevitable, therefore, that his contest with the enemies of his cause should assume occasionally a personal character, and that he should cherish toward them sentiments of disapprobation and hostility. It was natural also that in his oratorical campaigns, in seeking to gain adherents to the cause for which he pleaded, he should endeavor to communicate to his hearers the moral passion that fired his own soul, and rouse them also to indignation and hostility to these incarnate representatives of social injustice and treason. This emotional appeal may be carried too far and lead to heated controversies and denunciations which neither advance the true interests of a cause nor are worthy of its advocates. Mr. King cannot be pronounced entirely free from these rhetorical sins. But at most they were only incidental to his public discourse, and had much to justify them in the aims and conduct of the Secession party. It was no time for soft words and the discriminating and balanced consideration of rival principles and aims in the political order. The danger was imminent that the Federal Union would be dissolved, the State of California be made to join the Confederacy, and human slavery be established within its borders. The National flag had been fired on at Fort Sumter, a rebel army was marching on Washington. Every just oratorical appeal was in order which would maintain the loyalty of the state and nation and assure the supremacy of patriotic sentiments among the people. Never was such an issue presented to the latter for their solution. So far as the United States of America were concerned, the Civil War demanded of them a devotion, a sacrifice of life and of treasure greater than the Republic had hitherto known in its history. We justly take pride in America's great and altruistic contribution to a righteous decision of the world-war just ending. But the victory of justice, freedom and righteousness in the Civil War of 1860–5 has been the most important event in our career as a nation. Even a Pacifist like John Morley of England declares it to have been "One war which was justified by its results."

In what light Mr. King himself regarded this matter is disclosed by one of his patriotic discourses, "The Great Uprising." After emphatically declaring that it is the duty of a Christian minister to feel no personal animosity to any human being, he distinguished between a wrong done to himself and a wrong done to the community. He illustrates the distinction by a reference to the President of the Confederate States.[1]

"He is a representative to my soul and conscience of a force of evil. His cause is a pollution and a horror. His banner is a black flag. I could pray for him as one man, a brother man, in his private,

[1] E. P. Whipple's Memoir, p. 44.

[198]

affectional and spiritual relations to Heaven. But as President of the seceding states, head of brigand forces, organic representative of the powers of destruction within our country—*pray* for him! As soon as for antichrist! Never!" It would be, he added, incongruous to pray for him as he prayed for Abraham Lincoln. And he closed his sermon with the patriotic and devout utterance: "God bless the President of the United States, and all who serve with him the cause of a common country! God grant the blessing of repentance and return to allegiance to all our enemies, even the traitors in their high places! God preserve from defeat and disgrace the sacred flag of our fathers! God give us all the spirit of service and sacrifice in a righteous cause! Amen!"

Starr King's public activities for his country in that critical hour of its history teach with moving eloquence that there is a place and need for patriotism in the training of a human spirit, and that it is a mark of impoverished blood to deride it, even if it is but too often exalted at the expense of justice and truth by narrow and selfish advocates of "our country, right or wrong." It was one of the noblest implications of our Civil War that it should have stirred in the breasts of multitudes of men and women, to whom until that crucial hour disinterested and altruistic sentiments were comparatively unknown, a sense of personal duty to the common weal, a devotion to the ideals of liberty, justice and humanity, which lifted them above their own sordid interests and narrow sympathies into unselfish, heroic service for their country and their kind. The slogans of that day, the perpetuation of the National Union and the Freedom of the Slave, became their passwords of entrance into the brotherhood of man and the Kingdom of Heaven on earth. Many a man whom the customary appeals of religion had left unaffected found in patriotism an elevation of spirit, an ethical and humane impulse which led to his personal and social salvation.

The same thing is true of our recent world-war, and is one of the redeeming features of that terrible and lamentable conflict between the nations. It has mightily developed in modern society the National idea, which is a necessary stage in the evolution of a people. This National idea springs from the consciousness of descent from common stocks, from common traditions, interests and aims. It arises from the possession of a common country, language and literature, and common social and political institutions. All these make up that homogeneity of sentiment, that unity of purpose which constitutes a nation. An enlightened national patriotism, therefore, is one of the chief factors of civilization and the condition of moral and social progress. The history of mankind—from the Greek and Roman commonwealths down to the group of new nations that to-day in response to this sentiment have sprung into existence in Eastern Europe—impressively teaches

[200]

that only as this principle of Nationality is realized can any people become free, strong and prosperous.

Moreover, as Starr King would have told us, without this sentiment of loyalty to the Nation there can be no proper ascent to the larger conceptions of world-citizenship and world-brotherhood. As Mazzini said: "Nationality and humanity are equally sacred. To forget humanity is to suppress the aim of our labors; to cancel the nation is to suppress the instrument by which to achieve that aim." Society has expanded from devotion to clan or tribe to devotion to nation. We may believe that this will not be its final form. The existing state may in time give way to larger and wider forms of political organization. The proposed League of Nations points the way to a world-state, a universal brotherhood of mankind. But this last is a sublime Utopia which can be made actual only in a far-off and happier time, and then only by a natural and legitimate expansion of our national loyalties and duties. Nor is there any necessary conflict between patriotism and the love of mankind, between nationality and humanity, if we only see to it that our devotion to our country does not assume narrow, intolerant and unjust forms. Fundamentally the interests of individuals, of nations, and of the race are identical. It is only man's folly and wickedness that produce a conflict between them.

As the world-war reveals to us, love of country, love of nationality, is still a master passion of the

[201]

human heart. It is an inevitable and necessary stage in the evolution of human society, preparing the way for ever-enlarging conceptions of human brotherhood, of that new world in which nations and states will not be abolished but federated, and live together in peace and goodwill and service to one another.

This larger view of patriotism is well set forth in an oration on "The Organization of Liberty on the Western Continent," delivered before the Municipal Authorities of the City of Boston, July 4th, 1852.

This oration, written by Starr King in his 28th year, closes with an eloquent, and, in the light of recent events, remarkable presentation of the ideal aims of human society, a glowing prophecy of the New World which it is the privilege of the present generation to see arising out of the ruins of the old order, and in which justice, mercy, brotherhood and peace are to be the corner stones of a higher civilization; the precious fruits of an enlightened patriotism, whose ultimate aim is the redemption and uplift of the human race.

Said Mr. King:

"The mission of our land is still the path of organization, not aggressive propagandism or military interference. Let its influence be felt, in the lines of just and holy law, by process of construction through moral forces in favor of a higher national morality; by forcible protests against oppressive interference on the part of other nations in violation of the international code, but still with the dignity that shows the desire to keep the posture of peaceful friendship

[202]

and practical instruction towards the European world.

"Our responsibility to the oppressed of other lands is a deeper one than that of furnishing ammunition and supplies; it is the responsibility of faithfulness here to republican ideas, and of progress in the path suggested by the promptings of our history and the beckonings of Providence. Every noble institution we build up here is a more encouraging beacon to the struggling people of Europe than the fire-light of war. The striking off of each new fetter here resounds cheeringly through Europe. A musical tone travels much farther than a growl; and the effluence of a righteous victory of freedom on our shores will reach farther at last, and work more benefit for other races, than the sputter of our musketry in Trieste, and the roar of our floating batteries on the Danube. Let us not doubt that the wiping out of an oppressive statute in our code somehow makes the throne of Nicholas less firm. And all the prosperity, stability, and peace with which we invest the possession of freedom hasten the doom of foreign bondage, for they shed a light and a fragrance into the public sentiment that will guide the footsteps and revive the courage of the army of liberty in Europe, and they shame the lies that would brand republicanism as anarchy. . . .

"And so the lesson of our theme warns and beseeches us, as patriots and as lovers of the world, to go on in the work of organization. Our fathers have left us a work to do. We are no spiritual children of theirs if we believe that all which is desirable, and can be made safely operative in society, has been embodied here. Plainly enough there are unfinished portions of their scheme which it is for our

[203]

generation and those who come after us, to complete, out of reverence for their memory, adoration of the truth and love of mankind.

"If there is a race within our borders for which there is no organization of liberty, but upon whom the architecture of the Saxon institutions frowns like the sullen masonry of forts and jails; to whom their security is the security of the dungeon; and for whom the strength of law is the strength of bolts and chains: how plain is the call upon those of our people whose hands can help them, to consider their case in the light and by the methods of a practical and sinewy wisdom! . . .

"It is a problem of life, that may take generations perhaps to solve, but yet that must be solved, guided by the fixed principle that there must come the time when every human being who stands on American soil shall have rights that are hedged by friendly statutes, and a sacred freedom which the whole spirit of society is pledged to maintain.

"In whatever way the spirit of social justice can be made to enter more deeply into our policy, or domesticate itself in new features of our code without disruption of order,—in plans of land reform, —in adjustments of the relations of labor, so that the laborer may be more efficiently a man,—in the projection of schemes for the safety and nurture of the perishing classes,—we are called on cautiously to make the experiment; and to show how far and with what results the forces of society may shoot out into regions that have hitherto been abandoned to grim laws of competition and caprices of private charity. . . .

"Where is the American spirit that should be nurtured by our institutions, if, in the very light of

[204]

our history, we are to distrust the power of the people to organize better institutions for themselves than the brain of a tyrant can devise? Do you say that the path of revolution for Europe is a perilous and shaded way? We know it. But the last spirit to be fostered in the American breast is that which would bring all the perils that may beset the popular effort for self-government into any comparison with the quiet maintained by unscrupulous despotism. Institutions like ours Europe may not be able to establish, may not devise, may not desire; a long and bloody storm may intervene between the overthrow of oppression and the organization of peace; but it is not for us to preach and nourish hopeless distrust of the ability of popular Europe,— if left for a generation, or for half a century, in the experiment of liberty,—to correct mistakes, to prune excesses, and to find the preparation for republicanism which we so earnestly talk about, but which will never be gained by living under the shadow of absolute thrones.

"And finally, we are warned by our history not to distrust the capacity of the human race to attain a social order upon the earth of a higher stamp than any yet secured. It is *justice* which, thus far in human experience, has been heaving the foundations of society, that some of its principles may gain a solid place. The great struggle has been to balance the interests of the masses against the power of the few, so that nature might be, in some sense, a home for them, and existence a blessing. In the institution of such justice, at least for the white races, our land stands preëminent, far ahead of the nations that have gone before. Two centuries ago it would have seemed impossible, Utopian, to the

[205]

wisest statesmen and thinkers of the world, to realize on a scale such as this country now exhibits, such a scheme of self-supporting, orderly and stable democracy. But there are dreams of men, yes, promises of a wisdom higher than man's, that this earth is yet to be the scene of organizations nobler than those of justice,—organizations of *love*. It is inspiring to think of some far-off centuries as destined to witness the birth, the progress, and the completion of such a blessing for our race. And, looking at our condition from the cruel feudal times, or from the level of a Patagonian degradation, such an organization of love upon the earth does not seem wholly a dream. And so this great value belongs to our history, that the philosophy of it helps our Christian hope. It makes prophecy seem more sober. It brings the rhetoric of Isaiah within the sympathy of common sense.

"It is a summit from which the thinker may look off, like Moses from the mount, upon new and charming fields lying sweet in the smile of Heaven, where the armies of humanity—that have come up out of the bondage of despotism, and marched with sadness, but with courage, through the wastes and want of the desert of selfishness,—shall find a home, shall build amid plenty, and enjoy in peace; and the nations, bound into solidarity of life despite their varieties,—as the globe, with all its latitudes and zones, its polar and tropic climes, its mountains and prairies, its streams and seas, is organized into one physical republic,—'shall beat their swords into ploughshares and their spears into pruning hooks,' and praise the Creator through a life of song, labor, and prayer."

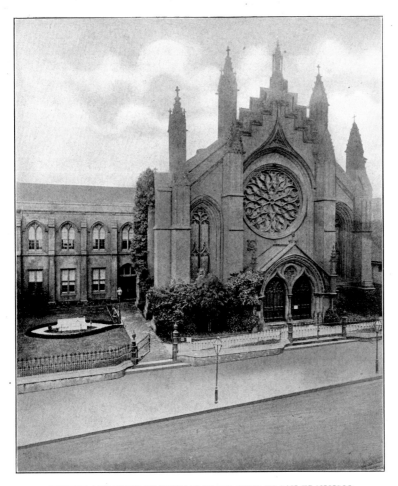

CHURCH AND TOMB OF THOMAS STARR KING IN SAN FRANCISCO

CHAPTER III

DEDICATION OF THE NEW CHURCH

RETURNING to Mr. King's ministerial duties we find him occupied with the completion of the new church his society was erecting.

Its corner stone was laid with appropriate exercises on December 3rd, 1862. Since no other clergymen of his own faith were on the Pacific Coast to assist him in the dedicatory exercises, Mr. King asked his colleagues on the Atlantic Seaboard to be present by letters or telegraphic message and share in the congratulation and joy of the occasion.

"Our new church will be completed about the last of July, and I wish to have letters read on the occasion from Bellows, Hedge, Dewey and Alger. Bartol will send a hymn, and perhaps Hedge also with his letter. So I hope, and so I trust you will urge them to respond. I do not ask for long and elaborate letters. A sheet of letter paper will be enough. We want the magnetic wire to connect us, that day, with the heart of the East. It will do us good to get shocks from all of you I mention. So do not fail to respond to this call for a little missionary labor. Write by the tenth of June, send by overland mail, and the letters will be in season. Do not delay after that."

[207]

He himself contributed over $5,000, to the undertaking, raising the money by lectures wrung from his over-worked brain. Mr. King felt that this was to be the crowning act of his life. "The new church completed and paid for," he writes, "I shall be ready to drop into my grave."

At length the handsome structure on Geary Street, since surrendered to the encroachment of business, was completed, and dedicated on Sunday, January tenth, 1864, in two successive services, to the Worship of God and the Service of Man. The hymn which the poet Whittier contributed to the service was especially admired.

Amidst these glorious works of thine,
The solemn minarets of the pine,
And awful Shasta's icy shrine,—

Where swell thy hymns from wave and gale,
And organ-thunders never fail,
Behind the cataract's silver veil,

Our puny walls to Thee we raise,
Our poor reed-music sounds thy praise:
Forgive, O Lord, our childish ways!

For, kneeling on the altar stairs,
We urge Thee not with selfish prayers,
Nor murmur at our daily cares.

Before Thee, in an evil day,
Our country's bleeding heart we lay,
And dare not ask thy hand to stay;

DEDICATION OF THE NEW CHURCH

But, through the war-cloud, pray to thee
For union, but a union free,
With peace that comes of purity!

That Thou wilt bare thy arm to save,
And, smiting through this Red Sea wave,
Make broad a pathway for the slave!

For us, confessing all our need,
We trust nor rite nor word nor deed,
Nor yet the broken staff of creed.

Assured alone that Thou art good
To each, as to the multitude,
Eternal Love and Fatherhood,—

Weak, sinful, blind, to Thee we kneel,
Stretch dumbly forth our hands, and feel
Our weakness is our strong appeal.

So, by these Western gates of Even
We wait to see with thy forgiven
The opening Golden Gate of Heaven!

Suffice it now.   In time to be
Shall holier altars rise to thee,—
Thy Church our broad humanity!

White flowers of love its walls shall climb,
Soft bells of peace shall ring its chime,
Its days shall all be holy time.

A sweeter song shall then be heard,—
The music of the world's accord
Confessing Christ, the Inward Word!

[209]

That song shall swell from shore to shore,
One hope, one faith, one love, restore
The seamless robe that Jesus wore.

Mr. King wrote his thankfulness and joy to a friend.

"SAN FRANCISCO, January 11th, 1864.
"My dear Alger:

"I seize the first moment that offers after the cares and joys of the Dedication to write to you greeting, thanks and friendship. . . . How long delayed our Inauguration has been! The Contractors and Architects promised us the Church in August last: they were four months behind time and they were tedious months to our Committee and myself. But we saw the church finished about Christmas and waited until we could get assurance that it would be paid for by subscription. We dedicated it yesterday.

"What a scene it was! It will hold fifteen hundred, and it was packed with souls that seemed to feel reverence and joy. A more beautiful church internally I never saw. The general arrangements were planned by myself, but the architect, Mr. Wm. Patton, a thoroughly trained English artist in Gothic, carried out the design with rare nobleness and taste. The whole cost is $90,000 for Church and Chapel and all appointments. We have just made a subscription in our city of $200,000 for the Soldiers' Sanitary fund, a large share of which comes from men interested in our movement. It was no boy's play to get 70 or 80 thousand dollars more for our church at Christmas time. But before the year is over—many say before a month—every cent will be paid. No mortgage will be allowed on

[210]

the building. We rent the pews for a year and obtained $20,000 in one night! Our plate collections are $5,000 a year. So that our income this year will be $25,000.

"We stand this year, I believe, in proportion to our pews No. One in the United States, so far as the amount voluntarily contributed for church expenses is concerned. Beecher raised $30,000 a year, out of a house twice as large. The letters from our Eastern brethren were a great feature of the dedication. I read them all, except Bellows', which was too long for the time at command, and will be read when the baptismal font his church has given shall be finished. All the letters were admirable. I never knew so hearty expressions of intellectual appreciation and grateful satisfaction as came to me at once after service yesterday, in response to your letters. Heartiest thanks for them.

"I long to get your book. How glorious is Martineau's article on Renan! I long to see you all. Gladly now would I surrender our exquisite church to a new man in all its prosperity, and let him enjoy the satisfaction of success. I begin to feel tired and lonely."

Mr. King was now led to think of rest and change of scene. The church was built, the State was safe, giving 30,000 majority for the re-election of Abraham Lincoln. Brilliant victories—New Orleans, Vicksburg and Chattanooga—had assured the permanence of the National Union. A remunerative investment in one of the Washoe silver mines, made on the advice of business friends in San Francisco, seemed to have rendered secure his own and his family's worldly fortunes. A journey to South America, a year of study thereafter in Germany, a work on the California Sierras, and one on Philosophy, were among his dreams. Yet through it all predominated the feeling that he should not live to realize these hopes. Mr. King was exhausted when he came to California, and the four years of his sojourn there were intensely exciting and wearing. Only by his powerful will and sense of patriotic duty had his frail body kept up its service until now. Like his father before him, he had always felt that he should not long survive his fortieth year, and it proved a true prophecy.

CHAPTER IV

DEATH OF THE PATRIOT AND PREACHER

IN the midst of plans for recuperation and future usefulness Starr King suddenly broke down. He attended on a Friday evening a social gathering of his parish. As he left the hall I observed his pallor and weakness, and entreated him to spare himself. On Sunday, February 28, 1864, his church remained closed and the report went forth of his sudden and serious illness. The physician, now called for the first time, pronounced it diphtheria, and said he should have been summoned at least a week earlier. It was evident that his illness resulted from the utter exhaustion of his physical system—he was dying from overwork, and for two days was barely kept alive. Pneumonia set in, but his wonderful recuperative power enabled him to resist this dangerous foe. But on Friday a second attack of pneumonia occurred, and his physicians gave up all hope of saving him. The story of his last hours is touching and beautiful.

When the second attack set in, Mr. King asked, "What is this? Is this pneumonia too?" His physician, Dr. J. N. Eckel, replied that it was. "Can I survive it?" Mr. King asked calmly. The doctor replied, "I fear not." "How long can I live?" "Not half an hour!" was the reply. "Are you sure that I cannot live longer than that?" asked Mr. King. The doctor replied sadly that he feared not. His sufferings now left him, and his voice, hitherto raised hardly above a whisper, responding to his will returned in full strength and power. Friends about his bedside inquired if he had anything to say. "Yes," he replied, "a great deal to say; first, I want to make my will." Calmly dictating his will, he had it read to him, paragraph by paragraph, saying "All right," at the close of each, and finally, "It is just as I want it." With a steady hand he signed his name in a handwriting as firm and clerkly as he ever wrote in his life, punctuating it and putting an accustomed flourish beneath it. After a few minutes of rest his friends came up one after another to bid him farewell. In every instance he greeted them with a pleasant smile, saying in his sweet tones, "Good-bye," and grasping their hands with fervor. To the maid, Sarah, he returned thanks for all her care for him, and commended to her his little son. He whispered to his wife, "Be sure and tell Dr. Eckel I think he has done everything a human agent could do." He sent a farewell message to his congregation: "Tell them it is my earnest desire that they pay the remaining debt on the church. Let the church, free from debt, be my monument. I want no better." To his wife he said: "Do not weep for me. I know it is all right. I wish I could make you feel so. I wish I could describe my feelings. It is strange! I feel all the privileges and greatness of the future!" "I see," he said to another, "a great future before me. It already looks grand, beautiful!" "Tell them at home," said he, "that I went lovingly, trustfully, peacefully." "To-day is the 4th of March. Sad news will go over the wires to-day." A moment of quiet ensued. Some one asking, "Are you happy?" he turned his full, bright eyes upon him,—"Yes! Happy, resigned, trustful." Thereupon in a clear, well-modulated voice he repeated the 23rd Psalm, "The Lord is my Shepherd,—I shall not want." At the words, "Yea; though I walk through the valley and the Shadow of Death, I will fear no evil; for Thou art with me; thy rod and thy staff they comfort me," he raised his finger with an accustomed gesture, and his voice was full of emotion. His little son was now brought to his bedside. "Dear little fellow! He's a beautiful boy," he said, and kissed his hand to the child as he was carried away. This was his last act on earth. Calmly closing his eyes his soul went forth into the great hereafter.

It is such a death as this that robs the grave of its terrors, and reinforces the oft o'erclouded instinct of immortality with the prophecy and assurance of eternal life.

The grief that followed the announcement of Mr. King's death was universal and unrestrained. A solemn hush seemed to have settled over the city which awoke as usual that morning to its restless and busy life. One by one the thousand flags that had fluttered so gaily in the morning breeze dropped half-way down, symbols at once of bereavement and com-memoration. The usual activity of business life was suspended. The Mint and other Government offices were ordered closed. The various district and local courts, after listening to brief tributes to his memory, adjourned for the day. The legislature of the State voted an intermission of three days. All felt it to be a national and not merely a local loss, and the sorrow even in the families that had never known him was all-prevailing and profound. On learning the sad intelligence, I went with a friend to his be-reaved home. Our German friend, Dr. J. N. Eckel, met us on the threshold. Said he, "I would will-ingly have died if it could have saved him." In the well-known parlor lay all that was mortal of our de-parted friend. It seemed peculiarly fitting that the flag he loved so well, and for which he had sacrificed his life as truly as if he had fallen in battle under its folds, should become his burial shroud.

It was only a few hours since his death, yet his features wore a contracted and rigid look as if from physical suffering. It seemed difficult to believe that this slight frame and worn countenance could have enshrined so great a soul. The poet Whittier nobly uttered the sentiment of the American community in that hour in his tribute to Starr King:

"The great work laid upon his two-score years
Is done, and well done. If we drop our tears

DEATH OF THE PATRIOT

Who loved him as few men were ever loved,
We mourn no blighted hope nor broken plan
With him whose life stands rounded and approved
In the full growth and stature of a man.
Mingle, O bells, along the Western slope
With your deep toll a sound of faith and hope!
Wave cheerily still, O banner, halfway down,
From thousand-masted bay and steepled town!
Let the strong organ with its loftiest swell
Lift the proud sorrow of the land, and tell
O East and west, O morn and sunset,—twain
No more forever! Has he lived in vain
Who priest of Freedom, made ye one, and told
Your bridal service from his lips of gold?"

The funeral service took place on the following
Sunday. A military guard had been placed to maintain order. Young men of the parish, the writer
among them, acted as ushers. When the doors of the
church were opened to the public a continuous stream
of people for hours flowed in and out of the edifice
to gaze once more upon the loved features of its minister, whose lifeless form lay at the foot of the altar
enshrouded by the American flag. On his breast
was a tiny bouquet of violets, placed there in compli-
ance with a telegram from Mrs. Jessie Fremont:
"Put violets for me on our dear friend who rests."

Never shall I forget the two negro women who
came forth with streaming eyes from the throng, and
kneeling by the inanimate form of this friend of their
race, with passionate sobs kissed the folds of the
United States flag which formed his burial shroud.

It was by the sacrifices of such heroes of the spirit that the Stars and Stripes had become to them also the emblem of liberty, the flag of *their* country.

The commemorative services were conducted by the Masonic body, of which he had been Grand Orator. Two large-hearted Orthodox ministers, a Presbyterian and a Methodist, assisted. With the organ, his gift to the church, sobbing a mournful miserere, with the triumphant song by a woman's voice: "I know that my Redeemer liveth!" and the afternoon sun sifting its rays through a stained glass window upon the preacher's lifeless form before the altar; with the booming of Government cannon from the adjacent square and Fort Alcatraz; with flags at half-mast from public buildings and the shipping in the harbor, while a vast crowd of twenty thousand people surged in and about the church, we bade him a last farewell on earth.

A telegraphic message sent from New York City by his friend Rev. Dr. Henry W. Bellows, President of the United States Sanitary Commission, best voiced the universal grief and sentiment of the hour.

"NEW YORK, March 5, 1864.

"To the People of California:

"The sad tidings of to-day have broken our hearts. Thousands here will weep with you over his bier. You have had our brightest, our noblest, our best, and he has lived and died, in the fulness of his manhood, in your service. Who shall fill his place on the platform, in the pulpit, in the hearts of his

friends? His full, quick, penetrative mind, winged
with fancy and with restlessness in the service of
truth, liberty and righteousness—his soul, glowing
with natural sympathy, Christian patriotism, universal philanthropy; his every action made to utter
and diffuse the noble, inspiring convictions of his
pure, loving nature; his eye the window of an open,
honest, fervent soul—his whole character, 'made
up of every creature's best'; strong and gentle, generous and prudent, aspiring and modest, controlling
and deferential; knowing the world and its ways,
yet clean of its stains; pious without sanctimony—
what but his own living, undying confidence in the
absolute goodness of God can enable us to sustain
such a measureless loss?

"The mountains he loved and praised are henceforth his monument and his mourners. The White
Hills and the Sierra Nevada are to-day wrapped in
his shroud. His dirge will be perpetually heard in
their forests.

"Farewell, genial, generous, faithful and beloved friend! Thou hast gone from those who
loved thee best. God comfort thy family, thy flock,
thy broken-hearted friends on both sides of a continent!"

On Sunday evening, April 3rd, 1864, there was
held in the Hollis Street Church in Boston an impressive memorial service to its former pastor, whom
the congregation four years previously had so re-
gretfully surrendered to the larger missionary needs
of the Pacific Coast. The beautiful edifice was filled
to overflowing with his admirers and friends. An
impressive simplicity characterized the proceedings,

[219]

revealing a grief that lay too deep for external expression. Loving hands had wreathed the pulpit with dark evergreens entwined with white immortelles, while across it was laid the silken robe of the departed preacher. The marble font below was filled with many-hued flowers, emblematic of his many-sided and radiant genius. The solemn music of the organ, the pathetic chanting of the choir, voiced the prevailing sentiment of the hour. The religious exercises were conducted by Mr. King's successor in the pastorate, Rev. George Leonard Chaney. In succession three of his most intimate friends, Edward Everett Hale, Edwin P. Whipple and Dr. E. H. Chapin, rose and paid eloquent and tender tribute to his personal gifts of mind and heart, and eminent public services.

The remains of the patriot-preacher, enshrined in a sarcophagus of marble, were deposited on the green plot by the side of the church edifice in San Francisco; for years an object of reverential regard to the passers-by and a place of pilgrimage for the admirers of Thomas Starr King.

STARR KING MONUMENT IN GOLDEN GATE PARK, SAN FRANCISCO

CHAPTER V

IN APPRECIATION

FROM whatever point of view we contemplate Starr King, whether as minister, orator, citizen, or simply as a man, we shall find much to admire, little to condemn.

Some men are eminent through their intellect, others through their conscience and courage, others still by their love and consecrated service. Starr King was notable in all these attributes of manhood. Few men were so free from faults or weaknesses. Says his intimate friend, Dr. Cyrus Bartol, "I abode with him by the month and never discovered a fault in him. I am profoundly ignorant, if he be a sinner, of the nature of his sins." Dr. Edward Everett Hale, William R. Alger, and others of his earlier friends have borne similar testimony. "Wherever he went," says his eulogist, Edwin P. Whipple, "he ennobled men. Meanness, bigotry, avarice, hatred, low views of public and private duty, all bad purposes and paltry expediences, sunk abashed away from the minds which felt the light of that sunlike nature. Everybody was more generous from contact with that radiating beneficence. Everybody caught the contagion of that cheerful spirit of humanity. Everybody felt grateful to that genial exorcist who drove the devils of selfishness and pride from their hearts and replaced them with high and generous sentiments."

His death elicited from Frank Bret Harte two poetic tributes. One of these: "Relieving Guard," with its beautiful imagery of a falling star, is well known. The other—"On a Pen of Starr King"— is a more personal and appreciative utterance and may appropriately be quoted here:

"This is the reed the dead musician dropped,
    With tuneful magic in its sheath still hidden;
The prompt allegro of its music stopped,
    Its melodies unbidden.

"But who shall finish the unfinished strain,
    Or wake the instrument to awe and wonder,
And bid the slender barrel breathe again,—
    An organ-pipe of thunder?

"His pen! what humbler memories cling about
    Its golden curves! what shapes and laughing
        graces
Slipped from its point, when his full heart went out
    In smiles and courtly phrases!

"The truth, half-jesting, half in earnest flung;
    The word of cheer, with recognition in it;
The note of alms, whose golden speech outrung
    The golden gift within it.

"But all in vain the enchanter's wand we wave;
    No stroke of ours recalls his magic vision;
The incantation that its power gave
    Sleeps with the dead magician."

IN APPRECIATION

Consider him as a patriot, and what nobler instance of devotion, of unselfish heroism is to be found in the annals of our Civil War? Though he died not on the field of battle, yet he gave his utmost to his country's need, and fell at last as true a martyr to the sacred causes of human freedom and national integrity as if he had dropped in the thick of the fight or wasted away in a military prison.

The service Starr King rendered his adopted State in her hour of peril has not been over-estimated. By his example and speech he did more than any other man, than any dozen men of his time, to lift the Pacific Coast to higher levels of patriotic duty and national sentiment. Not untruly did General Winfield Scott, commander in chief of the union armies, declare that Starr King had "saved California to the Union." It is known that President Abraham Lincoln was of the same opinion. And still his memory lingers among the mountains and valleys, the towns and mining camps of California, lending a lofty personal association to her magnificent scenery and romantic past, and preserving the tradition of moral heroism and patriotic service in the minds of her people.

Let us not forget what California did for him in return. It was in that new society that his genius, freed from the shackles of conventional thought and life, found its opportunity, soared to a higher circle of activities, and displayed its full maturity of power. His Eastern intimates were unable to understand how

[223]

one whom they had esteemed simply as a scholarly preacher and lecturer and a delightful companion, could disclose such remarkable abilities as a moulder of public sentiment, and become an idolized leader and inspirer of the masses, a heroic figure in our national history. "He was one of the last men," Dr. Henry W. Bellows confesses, "we should have thought of to spring to the helm in a time of public danger. He did not reveal himself to us as a man of action, a responsible leader of public opinion and a guide of practical affairs."

Amidst all our admiration for his eminent services to his country and his kind the thought intrudes how much more he might have accomplished if his life had been extended beyond the forty years allotted by Providence; what precious intellectual fruit might have been produced by his matured powers; what keen enjoyment to himself from the universal gratitude and love of his friends East and West and the Nation at large. But it was not to be, and we must rise to his own brave acceptance of destiny, and his lofty, unfaltering faith in the providential ordering of life and the eternity of the spiritual capacities of man.

His brief but brilliant career should teach high-minded and altruistic American youth how well worth while is the profession of a Christian minister; that no vocation offers greater opportunities for personal culture, ethical influence and public service, none confers such individual happiness or is more

[224]

widely useful in the community; especially in these latter days when more than ever the safety and welfare of human society depend on the larger acceptance of moral and religious ideals.

Henceforth Starr King's name and fame will be forever associated with California as one of the moral founders of that young and growing commonwealth, and a champion of the national idea among our American people.

There is no lack of fitting testimonials to the importance of the service he rendered. The printed tributes of his friends and admirers are many. A collection of his lectures and sermons, prefaced with a memoir by Edwin P. Whipple, was published in two volumes. Two grand mountain peaks, Mt. Starr King in the Yosemite National Park, and Mt. Starr King in his beloved White Hills of New Hampshire, uplift his name and fame into the region of storms and stars. One of the kingly giants of the forest in the Mariposa Sequoia Grove is also called after him. By the side of the present Unitarian Church in San Francisco stands, as it did by the earlier structure, the marble sarcophagus containing his ashes. The California Legislature has more recently voted to make Father Junipero Serra, founder of the early California Missions, and Thomas Starr King, its two representative heroes in the National Hall of Fame in the Capitol at Washington, and has made an appropriation for their effigies in marble for this purpose.

[225]

THOMAS STARR KING

In the great city park of San Francisco which overlooks the Golden Gate there was erected in 1892 by
popular subscription a bronze statue of Starr King,
lifting his endeared image against the sunlit blue of
a California sky, a constant reminder of his services
and an abiding incentive to equal patriotism and
devotion. The gifted sculptor, Daniel French, has
imparted such a life-like and spirited expression to
his work that it almost seems as if those bronze lips
must open with lofty and impassioned speech.

> "So let the light
> Stream on his deeds of love that shamed the light
> Of all but heaven, and in the book of fame
> The glorious record of his virtues write,
> And hold it up to men, and bid them claim
> A palm like his and catch from him the hallowed
> flame."